I'M A STRANGER
HERE MYSELF

OGDEN NASH

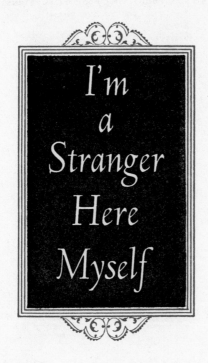

I'm
a
Stranger
Here
Myself

BOSTON

LITTLE, BROWN AND COMPANY

PRINTED IN THE UNITED STATES OF AMERICA

Some of these verses have appeared in the following magazines and are reprinted through the courtesy of: *New Yorker, Saturday Evening Post, Nash's, Titbits, Esquire, Life, Cosmopolitan, Fiction Parade, Harper's Bazaar.*

CONTENTS

· ix ·

· xi ·

· xiii ·

I'M A STRANGER
HERE MYSELF

Some ladies smoke too much and some ladies drink too
    much and some ladies pray too much,
But all ladies think that they weigh too much.
They may be as slender as a sylph or a dryad,
But just let them get on the scales and they embark on a
    doleful jeremiad;
No matter how low the figure the needle happens to
    touch,
They always claim it is at least five pounds too much;
No matter how underfed to you a lady's anatomy
    seemeth,
She describes herself as Leviathan or Behemoth;
To the world she may appear slinky and feline,
But she inspects herself in the mirror and cries, Oh, I
    look like a sea lion;
Yes, she tells you she is growing into the shape of a sea
    cow or manatee,
And if you say No, my dear, she says you are just lying
    to make her feel better, and if you say Yes, my dear,
    you injure her vanatee,
And in any case her eyes flow like faucets,
And she goes out and buys some new caucets.
Once upon a time there was a girl more beautiful and
    witty and charming than tongue can tell,
And she is now a dangerous raving maniac in a padded
    cell,
And the first indication her friends and relatives had that
    she was mentally overwrought

Was one day when she said, I weigh a hundred and
   twenty-seven, which is exactly what I ought.
Oh, often I am haunted
By the thought that somebody might some day discover a diet that would let ladies reduce just as
   much as they wanted,
Because I wonder if there is a woman in the world
   strong-minded enough to shed ten pounds or
   twenty,
And say There now, that's plenty;
And I fear me one ten-pound loss would only arouse the
   craving for another,
So it wouldn't do any good for ladies to get their ambition and look like somebody's fourteen-year-old
   brother,
Because, having accomplished this with ease,
They would next want to look like somebody's fourteen-
   year-old brother in the final stages of some obscure
   disease,
And the more success you have the more you want to
   get of it,
So then their goal would be to look like somebody's
   fourteen-year-old brother's ghost, or rather not the
   ghost itself, which is fairly solid, but a silhouette
   of it,
So I think it is very nice for ladies to be lithe and lissome,
But not so much so that you cut yourself if you happen
   to embrace or kissome.

There are two kinds of people who blow through life
    like a breeze,
And one kind is gossipers, and the other kind is gossipees
And they certainly annoy each other,
But they certainly enjoy each other,
Yes, they pretend to flout each other,
But they couldn't do without each other,
Because gossipers are lost without a thrill and a shock,
Because they like to sit in rocking chairs and gossip and
    rock and rock and gossip and gossip and rock,
And if the gossipees weren't there to give them a thrill
    and a shock their life would be all rocking and no
    gossip,
Which would be as flat as music without people named
    Sacha and Yehudi and Ossip,
While on the other hand everybody errs
If they think the gossipees could be happy without the
    gossipers,
Because you don't have to study under Freud or Adler
    or Coué
To know that it isn't any fun being a roué if nobody
    notices that you are a roué,
And indeed connoisseurs agree
That even gossipers don't know anything about gossip
    until they have heard one gossipee gossiping about
    another gossipee.
Another good thing about gossip is that it is within
    everybody's reach,

And it is much more interesting than any other form of speech,

Because suppose you eschew gossip and just say Mr. Smith is in love with his wife,

Why that disposes of the Smiths as a topic of conversation for the rest of their life,

But suppose you say with a smile, that poor little Mrs. Smith thinks her husband is in love with her, he must be very clever,

Why then you can enjoyably talk about the Smiths forever.

So a lot of people go around determined not to hear and not to see and not to speak any evil,

And I say Pooh for them, are you a man or a mouse, are you a woman or a weevil?

And I also say Pooh for sweetness and light,

And if you want to get the most out of life why the thing to do is to be a gossiper by day and a gossipee by night.

Oh, some people grieve for New Year's Eve
And some for the dog days fiddle;
My moment sublime is the restful time
When the month is at the middle.

Sing tirra lirra loo for the middle of the month,
Which wipes out woes like chamois!
The middle of the month is honey and milk!
The middle of the month is mammy!
Now let us exult,
For the bills of ult.
Are limbo's laughing stocks;
At Fate we scoff,
For a fortnight off
Are the impotent bills of prox.
The first of the month is oyster-gray,
The last of the month is clammy,
But it's tirra lirra loo for the middle of the month,
For the middle of the month is mammy!

Time, fly not back upon thy track!
The past is merely tedium,
And the future, too, so stand still, do,
While the month is at the medium!

Then tirra lirra loo for the middle of the month
And gambol it in like May Day!
The ravenous wolves are toothless now,
The lambs are in their heyday.

Now turn not pale
At the morning mail
Nor shrink when the telephone shrills,
No evil betides
On the blessed Ides,
The lull between the bills!
Oh, the first of the month is oyster-gray
And the last of the month is clammy,
But it's tirra lirra loo for the middle of the month,
For the middle of the month is mammy!

Carry me back to Ole Virginny,

And there I'll meet a lot of people from New York,

There the Ole Marsa of the Hounds is from Smithtown
 or Peapack or Millbrook,

And the mocking bird makes music in the sunshine accompanied by the rattling shaker and the popping
 cork.

All up and down the old plantation

Socialites are riding hell-for-leather like witches and war-
 locks,

And there is only one thing that keeps the squirearchy
 from being a genuine reproduction,

Which is that the peasantry's hair is kinky so they
 haven't any forelocks so they can't tug their forelocks.

In the evening by the bright light you can hear those
 darkies singing,

How the white folks do enjoy it and call the attention
 of their friends from Piping Rock to the natural
 musical talent of the dusky proletariat.

You can hear those banjos ringing because the hands
 have been ordered to exchange their saxophones
 for banjos,

And they wish they were singing Lookie lookie lookie,
 here comes Cookie, but their instructions are to
 sing Swing Low Sweet Chariot.

Oh what is more beautiful and more Southern than a
Southern beauty from Philadelphia or Rumson,
And indeed where was Southern beauty before the
advent of Schiaparelli and Elizabeth Arden?
And what is more gracious than a hostess calling you
you-all in the singular and plural indiscriminately,
And what has more local color than a lovely girl in
jodhpurs telling you about her gyarrrden?

Oh the long happy days spent huntin' or shootin' or
fishin',
Or in any other sport provided its lackin' in g's!
Oh the long happy evenings spent sniffing jasmine and
poring over the shiny new family Bible,
And figuring out that after all this is really your home
because great grandmother Wilkins was a Filkins
and the Filkinses were related by marriage to the
Randolphs or the Lees!

So please somebody carry me back to Ole Virginny,
Where gentlemen are gentlemen and a lady is known
by the product she endorses,
Where the atmosphere is as Southern as an advertisement for a medium-priced rye whiskey,
And where the Virginians from Virginia have to ride
automobiles because the Virginians from Long
Island are the only ones who can afford to ride
horses.

A CLEAN CONSCIENCE NEVER RELAXES

There is an emotion to which we are most of us adduced,
But it is one which I refuse to boost.
It is harrowing, browbeating, and brutal,
Besides which it is futile.
Because of it sleepy men go sleepless,
Because of it, for all I know lyrical canaries and night-
    ingales go peepless;
Hungry men lose their appetites;
Warm acrobats perspire coldly in their dapper tights;
Eligible bachelors enter ballrooms less eligibly,
And stoics talk to themselves loudly but fortunately also
    unintelligibly.
Land of Goshen,
What an easily dispensable emotion!
I am referring, of course,
To remorse.
Remorse is a violent dyspepsia of the mind,
But it is very difficult to treat because it cannot even be
    defined,
Because everything is not gold that glisters and every-
    thing is not a tear that glistens,
And one man's remorse is another man's reminiscence,
So the truth is that as far as improving the world is con-
    cerned, remorse is a duffer,
Because the wrong people suffer,
Because the very fact that they suffer from remorse
    proves they are innocuous,
Yes indeed, it is the man remorse passes over completely
    who is the virulent streptococcuous.

Do you think that when Nero threw a martyr to the
lions remorse enveloped him like an affinity?
Why, the only remorse in the whole Colosseum was felt
by the martyr who was reproaching himself for
having dozed through the sermon on the second
Sunday after Trinity.
So I think remorse ought to stop biting the consciences
that feed it,
And I think the Communist Party ought to work out
some plan for taking it away from those who have
it and giving it to those who need it.

BANKERS ARE JUST LIKE ANYBODY ELSE,
EXCEPT RICHER

This is a song to celebrate banks,

*Because they are full of money and you go into them
and all you hear is clinks and clanks,*

Or maybe a sound like the wind in the trees on the hills,

Which is the rustling of the thousand dollar bills.

Most bankers dwell in marble halls,

*Which they get to dwell in because they encourage
deposits and discourage withdralls,*

*And particularly because they all observe one rule which
woe betides the banker who fails to heed it,*

*Which is you must never lend any money to anybody
unless they don't need it.*

I know you, you cautious conservative banks!

*If people are worried about their rent it is your duty to
deny them the loan of one nickel, yes, even one
copper engraving of the martyred son of the late
Nancy Hanks;*

*Yes, if they request fifty dollars to pay for a baby you
must look at them like Tarzan looking at an uppity
ape in the jungle,*

*And tell them what do they think a bank is, anyhow,
they had better go get the money from their wife's
aunt or ungle.*

*But suppose people come in and they have a million
and they want another million to pile on top of it,*

*Why, you brim with the milk of human kindness and
you urge them to accept every drop of it,*

And you lend them the million so then they have two
million and this gives them the idea that they
would be better off with four,
So they already have two million as security so you have
no hesitation in lending them two more,
And all the vice-presidents nod their heads in rhythm,
And the only question asked is do the borrowers want
the money sent or do they want to take it withm.
But please do not think that I am not fond of banks,
Because I think they deserve our appreciation and
thanks,
Because they perform a valuable public service in elimi-
nating the jackasses who go around saying that
health and happiness are everything and money
isn't essential,
Because as soon as they have to borrow some unim-
portant money to maintain their health and happiness they starve to death so they can't go around
any more sneering at good old money, which is
nothing short of providential.

Dear Lord, observe this bended knee,
This visage meek and humble,
And heed this confidential plea,
Voiced in a reverent mumble.

I ask no miracles nor stunts,
No heavenly radiogram;
I only beg for once, just once,
To not be in a jam.

One little moment thy servant craves
Of being his own master;
One placid vale between the waves
Of duty and disaster.

Oh, when the postman's whistle shrills,
Just once, Lord, let me grin:
Let me have settled last month's bills
Before this month's come in.

Let me not bite more off the cob
Then I have teeth to chew;
Please let me finish just one job
Before the next is due.

Consider, too, my social life,
Sporadic though it be;
Why is it only mental strife
That pleasure brings to me?

For months, when people entertain,
Me they do not invite;
Then suddenly invitations rain,
All for the self-same night.

R.S.V.P.'s I pray thee send
Alone and not in bunches,
Or teach me I cannot attend
Two dinners or two lunches.

Let me my hostess not insult,
Not call her diamonds topaz;
Else harden me to the result
Of my fantastic faux pas.

One little lull, Lord, that's my plea,
Then loose the storm again;
Just once, this once, I beg to be
Not in a jam. Amen.

Once there was a girl named Miriam,

And she spent part of her time in a delirium,

And she said, I wish the world were a little less mysterious,

Because I do like to know when I am delirious,

But I have discovered that whenever I regard the world and judge it logical and normal and headed for the millennium at a mile a minute,

Why that's the time I ought to be enclosed in a spacious park with an asylum in it,

But whenever everybody else seems to be running around in a delirium,

Why that's the time when somebody may be fuzzy-minded, but it isn't Miriam.

So finally she convened an enormous convention, national and international,

And she said, Please I wish everybody would help me to determine when I am delirious and when I am rational,

Because, she said, at present I am just a bit hazy,

Because when I am crazy you all seem perfectly sane, but when I am sane you all seem perfectly crazy,

So, she said, forgive me if I am too personal or informal,

But I hope from now on you will all behave so that I will think you are delirious if I am delirious, and normal if I am normal,

So they all said, What a good idea, hurrah for Miriam!

Who are we? Who are we? We are the boys and girls
   of the Eastern and Western hemispheres, and we
   are going to help her with her delirium!
So from then on manias were declared reprehensible,
And everybody tried to be sensible,
And there wasn't any more war,
And there were only as many people dancing at night
   clubs as could comfortably get on the floor,
And all the rich people cried Soak the rich, and all the
   poor people cried No that would retard recovery,
   soak the poor!
And the tailors made men's and women's coats with the
   buttons on the same side, and that stopped a lot of
   argument between husbands and wives as to the
   comparative intelligence of men and women, you
   may be sure.
And what with one thing and another everybody was
   sensible and lived happily ever after and they said
   they owed it all to Miriam,
So they offered her the dictatorship of the world, but she
   never used it, only in a delirium.

I have been idly leafing through the Book of Proverbs
    and the Book of Deuteronomy,
But I have failed to find what I was seeking, which was
    a few pithy words on the subject of lovely woman
    and her weakness for peculiar economy,
And at first I couldn't understand the omission and
    then I thought, Why of course!
The Book of Proverbs and the Book of Deuteronomy
    were written before the days of Marconi and
    Morse,
And to appreciate lovely woman really entangled in the
    coils of economy you are unable
Until you have seen her in the coils of composing a
    telegram or a radiogram or a cable.
The occasion may be one of life and death, but she does
    not wire at once, she frugally decides to wait,
Because she is determined to save the pennies that are
    saved by getting the night or week-end rate,
So suppose you are out of town and your wife wants to
    tell you that the children have turned into wart
    hogs and somebody will give you a million dollar
    contract if you call them up right away and she has
    shot the minister's wife and eloped with the min-
    ister,
She will not squander money on a rush message, no, she
    sends it creeping overnight, thus saving a sum so
    tidy that you can't see it even in these days when
    the financial outlook is pretty sinister.

Or if by any chance the occasion is really important,
such as something to do with clothes, so that it
warrants a straight message, and hang the expense,
Why she leaves out so much trying to cut it down to
exactly ten words that it doesn't make any sense.
So this time suppose that she instead of you is out of
town and she decides that she should have brought
along a certain dress,
Why then she sends you a costly rush wire but she is
still economical and the instructions are so terse
that you have nothing to act on but a wrong guess,
So it takes about twenty dollars worth of electricity to
get straightened out and you are quite broke and
burst,
All of which could have been avoided if she had spent
an extra thirty cents at first.
Oh I often think that most of the misery in the world
is caused by the telegraph companies who make
you pay extra for all words over ten,
And I realize they have a right to a profit, but I wish
they would abolish all their present special rates
and start all over again with just one for lovely
economical woman, and one for men.

SONG BEFORE BREAKFAST

Hopeful each morning I arise
And splash the cobwebs from my eyes.
I brush my teeth and scrape my chin
And bravely at the mirror grin.
Sternly I force myself to say,
Huzza! huzza! another day!
Oh happy me! oh lucky I!
Another chance with life to vie!
Another golden opportunity
To rise and shine in this community!
Another target for my aim!
Another whack at wealth and fame!
Almost I feel within me stir
A budding force of character.
Who knows, indeed, but what I might
Perhaps have altered overnight?
Today may be the day, who knows,
That sees me triumph o'er my foes:
Gluttony, simony, and sloth,
And drawing on the table cloth;
Perjury, arson, envy, pride,
And renting tales of homicide;
Barratry, avarice and wrath
And blowing bubbles in the bath.
The differences this day may bring!
Perhaps I'll work like anything;
I'll travel to my tasks on foot,
And in the bank the carfare put,
And buy a haircut when I need it,

And if I get a letter, read it,
And every eve improve myself
With Pitkin or the Five Foot Shelf.
The things I want to do, I won't,
And only do the things I don't.
What lordly aspirations dawn
The while I draw my trousers on!
Oh beamish morning, big with hope
And noble tasks with which to cope,
If I should fail you, do not sorrow;
I'll be a better man tomorrow.

AN INTRODUCTION TO DOGS

The dog is man's best friend.
He has a tail on one end.
Up in front he has teeth.
And four legs underneath.

Dogs like to bark.
They like it best after dark.
They not only frighten prowlers away
But also hold the sandman at bay.

A dog that is indoors
To be let out implores.
You let him out and what then?
He wants back in again.

Dogs display reluctance and wrath
If you try to give them a bath.
They bury bones in hideaways
And half the time they trot sideways.

They cheer up people who are frowning,
And rescue people who are drowning,
They also track mud on beds,
And chew people's clothes to shreds.

Dogs in the country have fun.
They run and run and run.
But in the city this species
Is dragged around on leashes.

Dogs are upright as a steeple
And much more loyal than people.
Well people may be reprehensibler
But that's probably because they are sensible1.

Once upon a time there was a man named Orlando
Tregennis and he was in love with his wife,

And he thought he would express his love by serenading
her but his serenade wasn't very successful because
his playing interfered with his singing because all
he could play was the fife,

So then he said, I will climb the highest mountain in
the world and name it after my wife and then she
will give me a look of love, so he climbed the highest mountain in the world and his wife was indeed
whom he named it after,

But she didn't give him a look of love, she gave him a
look of laughter,

And not only a look of laughter but a look of menace,

Because he named it after his wife by naming it Mt.
Mrs. Orlando Tregennis,

So then he said that he certainly was sorry that during
the great war he had absent-mindedly forgotten to
join the army,

Because he said if he had been entitled to a bonus he
would have given her every penny even though she
was already so entrancing that no amount of mere
money could make her a jot or tittle more allury
or charmy,

And she greeted this remark with ribald merriment,

And she said that possibly money wouldn't get her any
further than she was, but she'd like a chance to try
the experiment,

So then Mr. Tregennis said, Well, I haven't any gold,

But I will give you my most precious possession, I will
give you my cold,

And he gave her his cold and first of all she tried to
spurn it,

And then she tried to return it,

But he said No darling, now it's your very own cold,

It is yours to have and to hold,

Because if you reckon I don't give gifts for keeps you
made a mistake when you reckoned,

Because there hasn't been an Indian-giver in the Tregennis family since my great-great-grandfather, old
Hiawatha Tregennis II.

But she wouldn't take no for an answer, but he wouldn't
say yes, and Mr. Tregennis's precious cold went
shuttling back and forth between them for the rest
of their lives,

And I hope everybody will turn out to be such self-
sacrificing husbands and wives.

Go hang yourself, you old M.D.!
You shall no longer sneer at me.
Pick up your hat and stethoscope,
Go wash your mouth with laundry soap;
I contemplate a joy exquisite
In never paying you for your visit.
I did not call you to be told
My malady is a common cold.

By pounding brow and swollen lip;
By fever's hot and scaly grip;
By these two red redundant eyes
That weep like woeful April skies;
By racking snuffle, snort, and sniff;
By handkerchief after handkerchief;
This cold you wave away as naught
Is the damnedest cold man ever caught.

Give ear, you scientific fossil!
Here is the genuine Cold Colossal;
The Cold of which researchers dream,
The Perfect Cold, the Cold Supreme.
This honored system humbly holds
The Super-cold to end all colds;
The Cold Crusading for Democracy;
The Führer of the Streptococcracy.

Bacilli swarm within my portals
Such as were ne'er conceived by mortals,

But bred by scientists wise and hoary
In some Olympian laboratory;
Bacteria as large as mice,
With feet of fire and heads of ice
Who never interrupt for slumber
Their stamping elephantine rumba.

A common cold, gadzooks, forsooth!
Ah, yes. And Lincoln was jostled by Booth;
Don Juan was a budding gallant,
And Shakespeare's plays show signs of talent,
The Arctic winter is rather coolish,
And your diagnosis is fairly foolish.
Oh what derision history holds
For the man who belittled the Cold of Colds!

Is anybody here in favor of a redistribution of wealth?

Because I think it ought to be redistributed, only not by force or by stealth,

Because it is only when other people have it and you haven't that it is evil,

So we had better try to correct the situation before it is made worse by a revolution or an upheaval.

Let us not be like the Soviets and fall prey to any communistic demagog,

No, surely we have more sense than a mujik and would yawn at arguments that keep them agog;

And let us not be sheep like a Fascist audience

Who get played on by their leaders like concertinas or accaudience;

Let us rather correct in our own 100% American way the wrongs that annoy and disgust us,

And correct them so the corrections will not offend the Constitution and Mr. Hughes, our imposing Chief Justice;

Let us handle it in the manner of Washington and Jefferson and Jackson

And keep very level-headed and Anglo-Saxon.

There are several things standing in the way of a natural distribution of wealth, but if you want to know which is the chief thing, well, I will tell you which:

The rich marry only the rich.

It is one of our national disasters

That, broadly speaking, Astors and Vanderbilts and Rockefellers and Morgans never marry anybody but

Morgans and Rockefellers and Vanderbilts and
    Astors,
Whereas if they only bestowed their affections on some-
    body in a lower crust,
Why money would be distributed over this broad land
    of ours like dust,
So I think they may all be rich but honest,
But I think their matchmaking proclivities ought to be
    harnessed.
Yes, if money marrying money were prohibited,
How speedily and how painlessly it would be redis-
    tributed.
Yes, yes, the rich and the poor can settle and forget their
    differences just as the Blue and the Gray have
As soon as we have a law saying that people can only
    marry people who have a lot less money than they
    have,
And that will be the end of all your present and future
    Townsends and Coughlins and Longs,
And that is why I call this piece the Song of Songs.

Some people are do-it-some-other-timers and other people are do-it-nowers,

And that is why manufacturers keep on manufacturing both bathtubs and showers,

Because some bathers prefer to recline

On the cornerstone of their spine,

While others, who about their comfort are less particular,

Bathe perpendicular.

Thus from the way people lave themselves

You can tell how under other circumstances they will behave themselves.

Tubbers indulge in self-indulgence,

And they loll soaking until they are a moist mass of warm rosy effulgence,

And finally they regretfully hoist themselves up and shiver and say Brrrr! even though the atmosphere is like an orchid-house and the mirror is coated with steam,

And they pat at their moistness with a towel as soft as whipped cream,

So it is obvious that the tubber is a sybaritic softie,

And will never accomplish anything lofty.

How different is the showerer, whose chest is often festooned with hair such as bedecked our ancestors arboreal!

He has no time to waste on luxuriousness, but skims through the spray with the speed of a Democratic politician skimming through a Republican editorial,

After which he grates himself on something which he
    calls a towel,
But which anybody covered with human skin instead
    of cowhide would call a file or a spur or a rowel,
And thus at the same time he avoids procrastination
And improves his circulation,
So we see that the showerer is a Spartan,
And sternly guides his ambitious life along the lines laid
    down by baccalaureate preachers and Bruce Barton,
And this is the reason that in the game of life although
    occasional points are won by the tubber,
The showerer always gets game and rubber.
Sometimes tubbers and showerers get into arguments
    about tubs and showers and become very warlike
    and martial,
But I myself have always been strictly impartial,
Yes, I am neutrally anchored halfway between Calais
    and Dover,
And all I will impartially and neutrally say is that there
    are three things you can't do in a shower, and one
    is read, and the other is smoke, and the other is
    get wet all over.

Barber, barber, come and get me;
Hairy torrents irk and fret me.
Hair and hair again appears,
And climbs like ivy round my ears;
Hair across my collar gambols;
Down my neck it wayward ambles;
Ever down it trips and trickles,
Yes, and where it trips, it tickles.
Barber dear, I wish I knew
Why I do not visit you,
Why I grudge the minutes ten
In your sanitary den,
Why I choose to choke on hair
Rather than to mount your chair.
Men no busier than I
Weekly to your office hie;
Men no braver than myself
Confront the armory on your shelf;
Men no wealthier than me
Gladly meet your modest fee,
And for a fraction of a dollar
Keep the jungle off their collar.
I alone am shy and flustered,
A solitary, cowardly custard,
Shaggy as a prize Angora,
Overrun with creeping flora.
Barber, barber, you're in luck;
The bell has rung, the hour has struck.
Sloth is strong, but hair is stronger;

I cannot stand it any longer.
Barber, barber, here I come;
Shake up the odorous bay rum;
Bring on your shears, your scythes, your snippers,
Bring on your crisp, electric clippers;
Employ a dozen extra sweepers;
Bring giant harvesters and reapers;
I warn you that a bumper crop
Waits to overwhelm your shop.
Barber, barber, be verbose,
Be anything, but clip me close;
Leave me razored, leave me scissored.
Leave me hairless as a lizard;
Barber, barber, singe and scald;
Barber, can't you make me bald?
I'd be the happiest of men,
And never think of you again.

FELLOW CREATURES

I

THE NEIGHBORS

The Frenches do not please the Germans,
Who call them names in hymns and sermons;
The Germans do not please the Frenches,
Who wish to shoot at them from trenches.
Now, anybody whom a German hates,
He presently exterminates,
But he who exterminates a French
Is never safe from Gallic revench,
But he who gets even with a German
Is obliterated like a vermin,
And so it goes for ages and aeons
Between these neighboring Europeans.
I hope that such perpetual motion
Stays where it started, across the ocean.

II

THE JAPANESE

How courteous is the Japanese;
He always says, "Excuse it, please."
He climbs into his neighbor's garden,
And smiles, and says, "I beg your pardon";
He bows and grins a friendly grin,
And calls his hungry family in;
He grins, and bows a friendly bow;
"So sorry, this my garden now."

THE NORTHERNERS

The folk who live in Scandinavia
Are famous for their odd behavia.
They have the frigidest of climates
And avoid their bellicose fellow-primates.
Though salesmen cluster at the door,
They don't want anybody's war.
It isn't that they put on airs;
They merely mind their own affairs.

IV

THE KING OF KINGS

The Emperor of Abyssinia
Had cousins in Harlem and Virginia.
And staunch supporters in Geneva
Whose strength was that of Little Eva.
A King of Kings and Conquering Lion
Whose land is full of oil and iron
Might just as well be Cousin Hetty.
I hope the Lion likes spaghetti.

You go into a store and select half-a-dozen shirts and
 charge them,
And finally you get them paid for along about the time
 you either have to give them away or enlarge them,
And you don't go back to the store because although it
 has nice shirts, still, for your modest budget it's
 rather expensive,
And the possibilities of a charge account are too exten-
 sive,
You need some more shirts,
But your conscience hurts;
Your bureau drawer is emptied
But you refuse to be temptied;
You say, No, they have nice shirts but they look on any
 purchase under two hundred dollars with boredom,
And I simply can't afforedom.
Well, everything is simply splendid,
And suddenly you get a letter from them saying they
 have been looking over their accounts and note
 that they have not served you since April 15th,
 1931, and in what way have they offended?
This is followed by other letters even more imploring,
Indeed the tone becomes positively adoring;
They beg you to purchase something from them,
They egg you to purchase something from them;
They hint that if their plea you ignore,
Why, they will simply close up their store,
And you succumb to their appealings,

And buy half-a-dozen shirts just so as not to hurt their
feelings.
Well, their feelings seem to recover all right from the
wreck,
Because around the middle of the following month you
get a letter from them saying they have been looking over their accounts and how about favoring
them with a check?
This is followed by other letters even more suggestive of
lovers' meetings ending in journeys,
And in about two weeks they turn over their share of
the correspondence to their attorneys,
So you send the check and the affair is ended,
And you swear off and in about a year you get a letter
from them saying they have been looking over their
accounts and note that they have not served you
since October 2nd, 1936, and in what way have
they offended?
Some people chase their own coattails in revolving doors,
And other people write letters for stores.

DON'T GRIN, OR YOU'LL HAVE TO
BEAR IT

It is better in the long run to possess an abscess or a
    tumor
Than to possess a sense of humor.
People who have senses of humor have a very good time,
But they never accomplish anything of note, either
    despicable or sublime,
Because how can anybody accomplish anything im-
    mortal
When they realize they look pretty funny doing it and
    have to stop to chortle?
Everybody admits that Michelangelo's little things in
    the Sistine Chapel are so immortal they have every-
    body reeling,
But I'll bet he could never have dashed them off if he
    had realized how undignified he looked lying up
    there with his stomach on the ceiling.
Do you think Der Führer could keep on being Der
    Führer
If he saw what everybody else sees every time he looks
    in the mührer?
Yes, fatal handicaps in life are fortunately few,
But the most fatal of all is the faculty of seeing the other
    person's point of view,
And if your devoted mother suggests that you will some
    day be rich and famous, why perish the suggestion;
That is, perish it if you are afflicted with the suspicion
    that there are two sides to every question.
Good gracious, how could anybody corner wheat

If they were sissy enough to reflect that they were caus-
ing a lot of other people to be unable to afford
to eat?

Look at mayors and congressmen and presidents, always
excepting college presidents, such as Harvard's
Conant;

Do you think they could get elected if they admitted
even to themselves that there was anything to be
said for their opponent?

No, no, genius won't get you as far as common every-
day facility

Unless it is accompanied by a conviction of infallibility,

And people who have a sense of humor are extremely
gullible,

But not enough so, alas, to believe that they are in-
fallible.

SONG FOR DITHERERS

I journey not whence nor whither,
I languish alone in a dither;
I journey not to nor fro,
And my dither to me I owe.
I could find a pleasanter name for it
Had I somebody else to blame for it,
But alas that beneath the sun
Dithers are built for one.
This is the song of the dither,
For viol, bassoon or zither,
Till the greenest simpletons wither
This is the song of the dither;
When regular troubles are wrong with you,
Others are guilty along with you;
Dithers are private trouble
Where you privately stew and bubble.
Come hither, somebody, come hither,
Would you care for a share of my dither?
I want somebody else to be mad at;
"Have at you!" to cry, and be had at.
I am tired of being angry at me,
There is room in my dither for three,
There is room in my dither for two;
We could butt at each other and moo;
We could hiss like the serpent, and slither
Through the tropical depths of my dither;
Like bees we could fight along beelines,
Or spit at each other like felines;
I care not who gaineth the laurel,

All I want is a foe and a quarrel.
Alone in my dither I pine.
For the sake of the days of lang syne,
For your white-haired old feyther and mither,
Come along, come along to my dither.
With no foe in my dither but me,
I swoon, I lay doon, and I dee.

People by whom I am riled

Are people who go around wishing O that Time would backward turn backward and again make them a child.

Either they have no sense, or else they go around repeating something they have heard, like a parakeet,

Or else they deliberately prevarikete,

Because into being a marathon dancer or a chiropodist or a tea-taster or a certified public accountant I could not be beguiled,

But I could sooner than I could into being again a child,

Because being a child is not much of a pastime,

And I don't want any next time because I remember the last time.

I do not wish to play with my toes,

Nor do I wish to have codliver oil spooned down my throat or albolene pushed up my nose.

I don't want to be plopped at sundown into a crib or a cradle

And if I don't go to sleep right away be greeted with either a lullaby or an upbraidal.

I can think of nothing worse

Than never being out of sight of a parent or nurse:

Yes, that is the part that I don't see how they survive it,

To have their private life so far from private.

Furthermore, I don't want to cry for the moon,

And I do want to hold my own spoon;

I have more ambitious ideas of a lark

Than to collect pebbles in my hat or be taken for a
    walk in the park;
I should hate to be held together with safety pins instead
    of buttons and suspenders and belts,
And I should particularly hate being told every time I
    was doing something I liked that it was time to do
    something else.
So it's pooh for the people who want Time to make
    them a child again because I think they must
    already be a child again or else they would stand up
    and own up
That it's much more fun to be a grown-up.

THE STRANGE CASE OF MR. DONNYBROOK'S BOREDOM

Once upon a time there was a man named Mr. Donnybrook.

᪥

He was married to a woman named Mrs. Donnybrook.

᪥

Mr. and Mrs. Donnybrook dearly loved to be bored.

᪥

Sometimes they were bored at the ballet, other times
at the cinema.

᪥

They were bored riding elephants in India and elevators
in the Empire State Building.

᪥

They were bored in speakeasies during Prohibition and
in cocktail lounges after Repeal.

᪥

They were bored by Grand Dukes and garbagemen,
debutantes and demimondaines, opera singers and
operations.

᪥

They scoured the Five Continents and the Seven Seas in
their mad pursuit of boredom.

᪥

This went on for years and years.

᪥

One day Mr. Donnybrook turned to Mrs. Donnybrook.

᪥

My dear, he said, we have reached the end of our rope.

✦

We have exhausted every yawn.

✦

The world holds nothing more to jade our titillated
    palates.

✦

Well, said Mrs. Donnybrook, we might try insomnia.

✦

So they tried insomnia.

✦

About two o'clock the next morning Mr. Donnybrook
    said, My, insomnia is certainly quite boring, isn't it?

✦

Mrs. Donnybrook said it certainly was, wasn't it?

✦

Mr. Donnybrook said it certainly was.

✦

Pretty soon he began to count sheep.

✦

Mrs. Donnybrook began to count sheep, too.

✦

After awhile Mr. Donnybrook said, Hey, you're counting
    my sheep!

✦

Stop counting my sheep, said Mr. Donnybrook.

✦

Why, the very idea, said Mrs. Donnybrook.

✦

I guess I know my own sheep, don't I?

෴

How? said Mr. Donnybrook.

෴

They're cattle, said Mrs. Donnybrook.

෴

They're cattle, and longhorns at that.

෴

Furthermore, said Mrs. Donnybrook, us cattle ranchers
    is shore tired o' you sheepmen plumb ruinin' our
    water.

෴

I give yuh fair warnin', said Mrs. Donnybrook, yuh
    better git them woolly Gila monsters o' yourn back
    across the Rio Grande afore mornin' or I'm a goin'
    to string yuh up on the nearest cottonwood.

෴

Carramba! sneered Mr. Donnybrook. Thees ees free
    range, no?

෴

No, said Mrs. Donnybrook, not for sheep men.

෴

She strung him up on the nearest cottonwood.

෴

Mr. Donnybrook had never been so bored in his life.

So this is bronchitis.

Well at least it is not appendicitis.

Well I suppose I ought to be thankful it's not bubonic
or pellagra.

Well I suppose I ought to be thankful I'm having it in
bed instead of floating in a barrel over Niagra.

And that is about all that can be said for it,

Particularly when you try to sustain life on what you get
fed for it,

And what you could do with the least of is what you get
the most of,

And that is something that is supposed to soothe your
throat and I don't see why it doesn't just glue it up,
and its flavor also is nothing to boast of,

And you drink water, water, water, and the only other
ingredient in it is sometimes soda and sometimes
aspirin,

And when your helpmeet approaches to help, you are
very grateful but you are afraid of giving her what
you have got, and a grateful embrace is the last
thing you can claspirin,

And if you smoke you increase your cough

But finally you decide you'd rather increase it than lay off,

And sometimes you are cold and that's a chill and sometimes you are hot and that's a fever

And all in all you are as merry as Danny Deever.

And if you try to read you go to sleep and if you go to
sleep you are waked up by somebody advancing on
your bedside without any stealth

And they poke a spoonful of something at you and tell
    you to swallow it and regain your health
And then you decide that if that is the only way to regain
    your health you just don't want to,
And then you begin to wonder who gave you your
    beautiful bonny bronchitis, and then finally you
    get to the fun of thinking who it would be fun to
    pass it on to,
And first of all for the good of humanity,
You'd like to give it to all dictators and political spell-
    binders of dubious sanity,
Because if they had bronchitis they couldn't spellbind
    and if they couldn't spellbind they couldn't dictate,
    and if they couldn't dictate they would have to stop
    going around with their jaws out or their right hands
    raised or their arms akimbo,
And they would sink back into their original limbo.
And something I should love even better than possums
    love persimmons
Would be to hand on my bronchitis to all singers who
    if they are women have voices like men's and if
    they are men have voices like women's.
Indeed the more I think of it the more I think gener-
    ously and altruistically though you may think I am
    thinking maliciously and boorishly,
Because I think I would like to give my lovely bronchitis
    both to almost everybody that sings or talks pro-
    fessionally, and absolutely everybody that sings or
    talks amateurishly,

And then, except for the sound of coughing, the day and
   night air would be quiet as it was before the birth
   of Marconi or Edison,
And now good-by thank you because I must explain to
   a woman that I don't need any more medicine.

Experience is a futile teacher,
Experience is a prosy preacher,
Experience is a fruit tree fruitless,
Experience is a shoe-tree bootless.
For sterile wearience and drearience,
Depend, my boy, upon experience.
The burnt child, urged by rankling ire,
Can hardly wait to get back at the fire,
And, mulcted in the gambling den,
Men stand in line to gamble again.
Who says that he can drink or not?
The sober man? Nay nay, the sot.
He who has never tasted jail
Lives well within the legal pale,
While he who's served a heavy sentence,
Renews the racket, not repentance.
The nation bankrupt by a war
Thinks to recoup with just one more;
The wretched golfer, divot-bound,
Persists in dreams of the perfect round;
He who despiseth the airwaves most
The modernest radio doth boast,
Hoping to find, through constant trial
One perfect program on the dial.
Life's little suckers chirp like crickets
While spending their all on losing tickets.
People whose instinct instructs them naught
But must by experience be taught,
Will never learn by suffering once,

But ever and ever play the dunce.
Experience! Wise men do not need it!
Experience! Idiots do not heed it!
I'd trade my lake of experience
For just one drop of common sense.

If I ever get to be a toastmaster,

Well, there is one toast I will never propose, and that
   is a toast to the Postmaster,

Or the Postmaster General, to give him his full title,

If you deem that vital.

I am sorry to sing off key in the harmonious choir,

But Postmaster Generals are something I do not admire,

Yes, it seems to me that an office of which the great
   American people need not boast

Is the office of the Master of the Post.

If I live from now till Doomsday or the Resurrection

I will never understand the affinity between the U. S.
   Mails and the next election,

The more so because as far back as I can remember,

Why, the Postmaster has been less interested in the post
   than in the first Tuesday after the first Monday in
   November.

You may think he is sitting in Washington brooding
   over a more efficient way of handling your postcard
   or letter,

But he isn't; he's out in Nebraska telling a lot of job-
   holders that if they haven't decided yet how they
   are going to vote, why if they want to hold their
   jobs, they'd damn well better.

Some Postmaster Generals have to buy new and bigger
   cars out of your money because their old car is too
   small to accommodate their topper,

And other Postmaster Generals graduate into the million-dollar job of preventing you from seeing any

movies that the Postmaster General mind considers not entirely proper,

And still other Postmaster Generals remember what they learned from Tammany,

Which is that Heaven may be reserved for the godly, but Earth is reserved for the Mammony.

Oh, dear, I certainly do wish there wasn't any law of libel or slander,

Because then I could say that I certainly do wish the Postmaster General didn't have to be a combination of the Lorelei and Machiavelli and Moses and Alexander,

Because I am very much interested in postmen, who bring you letters every day on their back in spite of snow and dust storms and rain,

And I am not at all interested in Postmaster Generals who instead of being interested in postmen are interested in the next, because they are the result of the last, campaign,

So therefore I make a plea for God, for country, and for Yale,

And I say in the future let us create a special Cabinet office for the man who has to get everybody re-elected, so that we can have a Postmaster General who can give all his attention to the mail.

THE MAN WITH TWO NEW SUITS

Who is that well-dressed handsome man?
Is everybody's eager cry,
I make response, for the fleeting nonce:
Excuse me, it is I!
The clangorous bells their homage pay,
The jubilant whistle toots,
And the murmur grows, Look there he goes,
The man with two new suits!

The first is a tasteful quiet gray,
The second is a quiet brown;
One wouldn't suppose such reticent clothes
Would so excite the town.
The coats display no waspish waist,
The trousers boast no pleats,
But the collars fit like Glyn and It,
And Oh the lordly seats!

On the gleaming steps of the City Hall
The Mayor takes his stand,
With welcoming teeth, and a laurel wreath
And a gold key in his hand.
The city is yours, the Mayor cries,
And the guard of honor salutes,
And the gaping crowd cheers long and loud
For the man with two new suits.

The brown one has a single breast,
And the breast of the gray is double,

And they mold the form to the perfect norm
Where the scapulae cease to trouble.
The trousers nestle around the hips,
Then flow like a weeping willow —
Oh as gay am I as a butterfly,
Yet snug as the armadillo!

The old suit bagged across the knees,
And it also bagged behind;
The foraging moth had pierced its cloth,
And the nap was neatly shined.
I gave that suit to a shabby tramp,
I thought his poverty earned it,
And he said What's that? And then he spat,
And he took it out and burned it.

But now bring forth your noblest malt,
Your noblest barley and grape,
Triumphal parade and cavalcade
And torrent of ticker tape!
Now man and child shall work no more,
But seize their zithers and lutes,
And spend their days in endless praise
Of the man with two new suits!

Oh, sometimes I wish I had the wings of an angel
because then I could fly through the air with the
greatest of ease,

And if I wanted to be somewhere else I could get there
without spending any money on taxis or railroad
tickets or tips or fees,

Yes, I could fly to Paris and do as a Parisian, or fly to
Rome and do as a Roman,

But on the other hand wings would necessitate my
sleeping on my abdomen,

So I don't really wish I had the wings of an angel, but
sometimes I wish I had the sweet voice of a thrush,

And then if I sang an Indian Love Lyric why thou-
sands of beautiful beauties would harken and
quiver and blush,

And it would be a treat to hear my rendition of
Sweet Alice Ben Bolt,

But on the other hand who would go to harken to
anybody who was known to eat insects and moult?

So I don't really wish I had the sweet voice of a thrush,
but sometimes I wish I had the courage of a lion,

And then I could look life in the eye with a will of
iron,

And to a goose, or a burglar, or even a butler, I wouldn't
hesitate to say Boo!

But on the other hand I might encounter a goose or a
burglar or a butler who had the courage of a lion
too,

So I don't really wish I had the courage of a lion but
   sometimes I wish I had an elephant's muscle,
And then when somebody fainted or got run over I
   could always get in the front row of spectators no
   matter how thick the hustle and bustle,
But on the other hand I would probably find myself
   in some job where such strength would be utilita-
   rian,
So if I had the muscle of an elephant, why instead of
   of lying back comfortably and wishing I had the
   muscle of an elephant, why I would probably be
   busy building a tower in Manhattan or tunneling
   through a peak in Darian,
So I don't really wish I had the muscle of an elephant
   but sometimes I wish I had the innocence of a
   lamb,
And then I would never wake up crying Fie on me!
   and Damn!
But on the other hand innocence is a security on which
   it is hard to borrow,
Because all it means is that either you get eaten by a
   wolf today or else the shepherd saves you from
   the wolf so he can sell you to the butcher tomorrow,
So I do not really wish I had the innocence of a lamb,
I guess I'll stay just as I am.

TO A LADY PASSING TIME BETTER LEFT
UNPASSED

O lady of the lucent hair,
Why do you play at solitaire?
What imp, what demon misanthrope,
Prompted this session of lonely hope?
What boredom drives you, and great Lord!
How can such as you be bored?
The gleaming world awaits your eye
While you essay futility.
That mouth is shaped for livelier sport
Than paging of a pasteboard court —
Why, even the Red Knave longing lingers,
While Black Queens wait, in those white fingers. —
See now the joy that lights your face
Squandered on some fortuitous ace,
Where formerly dark anger burned
When a five perverse would not be turned.
O, know you not, that darkling frown
Could topple Caesar's empire down;
That quick, bright joy, if flashed on men,
Could sudden build it up again?
Get up! Get up! Throw down the pack!
Rise in your gown of shining black!
Withdraw, my dear, while you are able
The slender feet from neath the table;
Remove from the regretful baize
The elbows curved in cunning ways.
Is there no game that pleasure brings
But fretting over painted things?

No gay, ecstatic end in view
But shuffle and begin anew?
Get up, I tell you, girl, get up!
Wine keeps not ever in the cup;
Music is mortal, comes a day
When the musicians will not play;
Even Love immortal, love undying,
Finds the loved one's Patience trying.
Let two-and-fifty rivals hiss me —
For God's sake, girl, come here and kiss me!

THE STRANGE CASE OF THE BLACKMAILING DOVE

Once upon a time there was a flock of doves.

∽

They used to sit around the dovecote and coo.

∽

The littlest dove was named Daingerfield.

∽

Daingerfield could coo like the dickens, but he never got anything to eat.

∽

Whenever anything to eat turned up, the buxom doves elbowed him out of the way.

∽

The buxom doves got buxomer and buxomer.

∽

Daingerfield got tenuouser and tenuouser.

∽

Meanwhile he kept on cooing.

∽

One day his mind was weakened by starvation and he forgot his lines.

∽

He didn't say Coo.

∽

He said Boo.

∽

The buxom doves were panic-stricken. They fluttered around him like doves.

∽

Daingerfield knows all, said the buxom doves. But good
old Daingerfield won't tell, will you Daingerfield?

~

Boo, said Daingerfield.

~

Thenceforth the buxom doves presented the daintiest
titbits to Daingerfield.

~

This is the life, he thought.

~

Boo, he said. Who's holding out on a titbit? Boo!

~

After a while the doves were invited to a society wedding.

~

It was the wedding of Felise Bankery, only child of Mrs.
Liz Bankery Brokery Buttery and the late Reginald
Bankery, the noted runner-up.

~

Felise was to marry the dashing Borogavian mixed triples
runner-up, Baron Von Luciano.

~

Mrs. Liz Bankery Brokery Buttery thought a flock of
doves in the church would be nice.

~

Different, she said, and sort of symbolic.

~

The doves were released as the happy pair stood at the
altar.

~

The cathedral echoed with their cooing.

❧

Daingerfield couldn't see a thing. He sulked until the cooing stopped.

❧

Boo! said Daingerfield clearly.

❧

The bride jumped. So did the groom. Then they beckoned to Daingerfield.

❧

This is soft, thought Daingerfield. He approached, booing mellifluously.

❧

Why do you boo? asked Felise. Is it because of the brace and a half of twins ensuing from my secret marriage to the chauffeur?

❧

Boo, said Daingerfield with a smirk.

❧

Why do you boo? asked Baron Von Luciano. Is it because the social position of a baron in Borogavia is that of an extra waiter at a banquet?

❧

Boo, said Daingerfield with another smirk.

❧

The bride turned to the groom.

❧

After all, she said simply, a baron is a baron, and we don't have to go to Borogavia, do we?

❧

The groom turned to the bride.

∞

After all, he said, a hundred million is a hundred million,
and we can fire the chauffeur, can't we?

∞

No indeed, said the bride.

∞

Coo, said Daingerfield.

The country is a funny place,
I like to look it in the face.
And everywhere I look I see
Some kind of animal or tree.

Indeed, I frequently remark
The country is rather like a park.

The country cows give milk, and moo,
Just like their sisters in the zoo.
The rural squirrel in his rage
Chirks like a squirrel in a cage.

Animals, in their joys and passions,
Like women, follow city fashions.

The horses here pull plows and carts
All day until the sun departs.
In summer, or when fields are frosted,
They work until they are exhausted.

Next, to the track themselves they hie
To be bet upon by the likes of I.

As through the countryside you pass
You look at grass and still more grass.
Grass leers at you where'er you turn
Until your tired eyelids burn.

They ought to break it up, or soften it,
With pretty signs saying, please keep offen it.

I like the country very much.
It's good to hear and smell and touch.
It makes you feel akin with Nature,
Though wobbly on her nomenclature.

I'd free my lungs of city air
If I didn't feel much more important there.

Monday is the day that everything starts all over again,

Monday is the day when just as you are beginning to feel peaceful you have to get up and get dressed and put on your old gray bonnet and drive down to Dover again,

It is the day when life becomes grotesque again,

Because it is the day when you have to face your desk again;

It is a day with no fun about it,

Because it is the first of a series of days filled with one task or another that something has to be done about it.

When the telephone rings on Saturday or Sunday you are pleased because it probably means something pleasing and you take the call with agility,

But when it rings on any other day it just usually means some additional responsibility,

And if in doubt,

Why the best thing to do is to answer it in a foreign accent or if you are a foreigner answer it in a native accent and say you are out.

Oh, there is not a week-day moment that can't wring a sigh from you,

Because you are always being confronted with people who want to sell you something, or if they don't want to sell you something, there is something they want to buy from you,

And every shining hour swaggers arrogantly up to you demanding to be improved,

And apparently not only to improve it, but also to shine
    it, is what you are behooved.
Oh for a remedy, oh for a panacea, oh for a something,
    oh yes, oh for a coma or swoon,
Yes indeed, oh for a coma that would last from nine
    A.M. on Monday until Saturday noon.

POOR MR. STRAWBRIDGE

Once there was a man named Mr. Strawbridge,
And all he wanted was a drawbridge,
But when people asked him what kind
He couldn't make up his mind.
His fingernails he would bite and his thumbs he would
    twiddle
Trying to decide whether he wanted one that revolved
    on a pivot or one that went up in the middle,
So finally everybody went to Mr. Strawbridge
And asked him why he wanted a drawbridge.
And Mr. Strawbridge smiled a smile seraphic
And said he wanted it because he wanted to interfere
    with traffic.
He said that on his house he had a veranda built,
And it was comfortable enough for a Vanderbilt,
And he said it gave him great satisfaction
To sit on his veranda and watch the Atlantic Ocean in
    action
But he said sometimes on Sundays and holidays he
    couldn't see the Atlantic for the motorists,
And he said he'd rather see the former than the latter
    even though they were handsome and respectable
    Kiwanians and Lions and Rotarists,
And he said maybe he was a silly old goose,
But it always gave him a pain to see a line of automo-
    biles practically hooked up together like freight cars
    on a long freight train, particularly when the
    freight train was ten miles long and you never
    seemed to get to the caboose,

And he said that doubtless all that gipsying was most
	romantic,
But he still preferred looking at the Atlantic
And he said he didn't see why people went out in one
	automobile between a lot of other automobiles, be-
	cause they didn't get any air or scenery,
No, they just got a view of the license plate in front
	and a lot of annoyance and dust and gasolinery,
And therefore, said Mr. Strawbridge,
Everybody else would see just as much and I would see
	much more if they were all held up somewhere by
	an open drawbridge,
So all his friends said he was a genius,
And they gave him a lot of orchids and gardenius,
But they never gave him a drawbridge,
And that is why I call him poor Mr. Strawbridge.

A gentlemanly gentleman, as mild as May,
Entered a restaurant famed and gay.
A waiter sat him in a draughty seat
And laughingly inquired what he'd like to eat.
"Oh I don't want venison, I don't want veal,
But I do insist on coffee with the meal.
Bring me clams in a chilly group,
And a large tureen of vegetable soup,
Steak as tender as a maiden's dream,
With lots of potatoes hashed in cream,
And a lettuce and tomato salad, please
And crackers and a bit of Roquefort cheese,
But waiter, the gist of my appeal,
Is coffee with, coffee with, coffee with the meal."
The waiter groaned and he wrung his hands;
"Perhaps da headwaiter onderstands."
Said the sleek headwaiter, like a snobbish seal,
"What, monsieur? Coffee with the meal?"
His lip drew up in scornful laughter;
"Monsieur desires a demi-tasse after!"
Monsieur's eyes grew hard as steel,
He said, "I'm ordering coffee with the meal.
Hot black coffee in a great big cup,
Fuming, steaming, filled right up.
I don't want coffee iced in a glass,
And I don't want a miserable demi-tasse,
But what I'll have, come woe, come weal,
Is coffee with, coffee with, coffee with the meal."
The headwaiter bowed like a poppy in the breeze;

"Monsieur desires coffee with the salad or the cheese?"
Monsieur said, "Now you're getting warmer;
Coffee with the latter, coffee with the former;
Coffee with the steak, coffee with the soup,
Coffee with the clams in a chilly group;
Yes, and with a cocktail I could do,
So bring me coffee with the cocktail, too.
I'll fight to the death for my bright ideal,
Which is coffee with, coffee with, coffee with the meal."
The headwaiter swiveled on a graceful heel;
"Certainly, certainly, coffee with the meal!"
The waiter gave an obsequious squeal,
"Yes sir, yes sir, coffee with the meal!"
Oh what a glow did Monsieur feel
At the warming vision of coffee with the meal.
One hour later Monsieur, alas!
Got his coffee in a demi-tasse.

THE QUEEN IS IN THE PARLOR

Let's go over to Lily's,
And we'll all play games;
We'll act like regular sillies,
We'll assume ridiculous names,
We'll embarrass the butler,
And shock the maids,
With some of our subtler
Sly charades.
Come along, come along to Lily's,
Effervescent incessantly Lily's,
Come along, come along to Lily's,
And we'll all play games.

Lily is loaded with strictures
And many a palpable hit
For people who won't draw pictures,
For people who won't be IT.
There are sharpened pencils
And virgin papers,
All the utensils
For mental capers.
Here's a new one! You're going to love it!
Just enter into the spirit of it!
The name of the game is, Who Is Whom?
Harold, you have to leave the room;
I hope a few minutes alone won't bore you;
We'll whistle when we are ready for you.
Amanda, sit on the chandelier;
You represent Eternity, dear;

Now let me think — oh yes, Louise,
Stand on the sofa — on one leg, please;
You're Nelson — oh, it was Nelson's arm!
Well, a change of limbs lends whimsical charm.
George and Edward are Scrooge and Marley;
Pincus, you be Bonnie Prince Charlie.
Now, do I dare be Cleopatra?
No, really I don't! Why George, you flattra!
Everyone ready? This is fun!
Harold must guess us, every one,
And portray us all in a cartoon trim
While we each write a sonnet on him.
Hoo hoo, Harold! Hoo hoo! Hoo hoo!
Come in now, Harold, we're ready for you!
Hoo hoo, Harold! — Oh no! Not that!
Harold is missing, and so's his hat.

Let's go over to Lily's,
We'll all play games;
We'll bloom like daffy-down-dillies
And romp like Colonial Dames.
Anne, think of a number!
George, pick a card!
But I shall slumber
And slumber hard.
Come along, come along to Lily's,
Energetic aesthetically Lily's
Come along, come along to Lily's,
The Queen of the Parlor Games!

Breakfast is an institution that I don't know who com-
   menced it,
But I am not for it, I am against it.
It is a thoroughly inedible repast,
And the dictionary says it is derived from the words
   break, meaning to break, and fast, meaning a fast,
   so to breakfast means to break your fast.
Well that just shows how far you can trust a dictionary,
Because I never saw a definition that was more utterly
   fictionary.
The veriest child could see it doesn't check,
Because if the first syllable of breakfast means to break,
   why is it pronounced brek?
Shame on you, you old lexicographers, I shall call you
   laxicographers because you have grown very lax,
Because it is perfectly obvious that the first syllable in
   breakfast is derived from the far-famed Yale foot-
   ball cheer, which is Brekekekex co-ax co-ax,
And did you even get the second syllable right? Why a
   thousand times No,
Because the fast in breakfast doesn't mean fast, absti-
   nence from food, it means fast, not slow.
So with that in mind we can peek behind the scenes
And then we can see what break-fast really means,
It means that if you wake up in the morning feeling un-
   appetized and sickly,
Why you are confronted by a meal and the entire Yale
   football team coaxes you with an axe to eat it
   quickly.

On this topic I could write a chapter,

But I will content myself with saying that the French
  word for breakfast, which is dejeuner, is consid-
  erably apter,

Because it is perfectly truthful,

Because it is made up of the words de, meaning to un-
  something, and jeuner, which must be derived from
  the word jeune, meaning young, so jeuner must
  mean to grow youthful,

So I think that is the reason that the French are always
  bright and gay,

Because they never eat breakfast because they are warned
  off it by their word for it, which means something
  that if you eat it you will grow unyouthful right
  away.

THE STRANGE CASE OF MR. BALLANTINE'S
VALENTINE

Once upon a time there was an attorney named Mr.
Ballantine.

~

He lived in the spacious gracious days of the nineteenth
century.

~

Mr. Ballantine didn't know they were spacious and
gracious.

~

He thought they were terrible.

~

The reason he thought they were terrible was that love
had passed him by.

~

Mr. Ballantine had never received a valentine.

~

He said to his partner, My name is Mr. Ballantine and
I have never received a valentine.

~

His partner said, Well my name is Mr. Bogardus and I
have received plenty of valentines and I just as
soon wouldn't.

~

He said Mr. Ballantine didn't know when he was well
off.

~

Mr. Ballantine said, I know my heart, I know my mind,
I know I long for a valentine.

~

He said here it was St. Valentine's day and when he
   sat down at his desk what did he find?

∽

Valentines?

∽

No.

∽

I find affidavits, said Mr. Ballantine.

∽

That's the kind of valentine I get, said Mr. Ballantine.

∽

Mr. Bogardus said that affidavit was better than no
   bread.

∽

Mr. Ballantine said that affidavit, affidavit, affidavit on-
   ward, into the valley of death rode the six hun·
   dred.

∽

Mr. Bogardus said that any man who would rhyme "on-
   ward" with "six hundred" didn't deserve any affi·
   davits at all.

∽

Mr. Ballantine said coldly that he was an attorney, not
   a poet, and Mr. Bogardus had better take the matter up directly with Lord Tennyson.

∽

Mr. Bogardus said Oh all right, and speaking of lords,
   he couldn't remember who was the king before
   David, but Solomon was the king affidavit.

∽

Mr. Ballantine buried Mr. Bogardus in the cellar and
   went out in search of love.

∽

Towards evening he encountered a maiden named Herculena, the Strongest Woman in the World.

∽

He said, Madam my name is Mr. Ballantine and I have never received a valentine.

∽

Herculena was delighted.

∽

She said, My name is Herculena the Strongest Woman in the World, and I have never received a valentine either.

∽

Mr. Ballantine and Herculena decided to be each other's valentine.

∽

All was merry as a marriage bell.

∽

Mr. Ballantine nearly burst with joy.

∽

Herculena nearly burst with pride.

∽

She flexed her biceps.

∽

She asked Mr. Ballantine to pinch her muscle.

∽

Mr. Ballantine recovered consciousness just in time to observe the vernal equinox.

∽

He thought she said bustle.

EPILOGUE TO MOTHER'S DAY, WHICH IS TO BE PUBLISHED ON ANY DAY BUT MOTHER'S DAY

Mothers! Mothers! It was visions of mothers that had
    been relentlessly haunting me,
Wherever I turned I saw misty mothers sitting around
    taunting me.
It was battalions of irritated spectres that blanched my
    face and gave me this dull and lustre-lack eye,
Night and day I was surrounded by mothers, from Mrs.
    Whistler, Senior, to Mrs. Dionne and from Yale
    the mother of men to Niobe and the mother of
    the Gracchi.
I resented this supernatural visitation, these are not the
    dark ages, these are the days of modernity,
I wilted before this intrusion of miasmic maternity.
Mothers, I cried, oh myriads of mothers, I can stand
    it no longer, what can I do for you?
Do you want me to have you excorcised, do you want
    me to pray for you, do you want me to say Boo
    for you?
I know you are major figures in history's Who's Whom,
But I wish you would go away because your company
    is flattering but I would rather have your room.
Then they replied in hollow chorus,
We have thought of something that we want to have
    published but we can't write so you will have to
    write it for us,
And if you write it we will leave you alone,

And if you don't write it we will haunt you brain from
    skull and flesh from bone,
So I acquiesced and the ghastly horde dictated to me
    and I wrote it,
And a promise is a promise and an army of ghostly
    mothers is an army of ghostly mothers, so I quote
    it: —
M is for the preliminary million-dollar advertising ap-
    propriation,
O means that she is always white-haired, bespectacled
    and at least eighty-five years old,
T is for Telegraph message number 31B which con-
    tains a tastefully blended expression of sentiment
    and congratulation,
H is for the coast-to-coast questionnaire which proved
    conclusively that seven-and-one-half citizens out
    of every ten with incomes of $5000 a year or better
    would rather have their mother than gold.
E is for the Elephants which everybody is very glad
    didn't sit down on their mothers,
R is for Rosemary which is for Remembrance of the
    fact that a mother is one thing that you will never
    have more than one of,
Put them all together and before you can say H. St. C.
    Wellington Carruthers, they spell the second of
    two things that everybody who loves their mother
    only once a year and then only at the instigation
    of the Chamber of Commerce is a son of.

Let us pause to consider the English,

Who when they pause to consider themselves they get
all reticently thrilled and tinglish,

Because every Englishman is convinced of one thing,
viz.:

That to be an Englishman is to belong to the most ex-
clusive club there is:

A club to which benighted bounders of Frenchmen and
Germans and Italians et cetera cannot even aspire
to belong,

Because they don't even speak English, and the Ameri-
cans are worst of all because they speak it wrong.

Englishmen are distinguished by their traditions and
ceremonials,

And also by their affection for their colonies and their
contempt for their colonials.

When foreigners ponder world affairs, why sometimes
by doubts they are smitten,

But Englishmen know instinctively that what the world
needs most is whatever is best for Great Britain.

They have a splendid navy and they conscientiously
admire it,

And every English schoolboy knows that John Paul
Jones was only an unfair American pirate.

English people disclaim sparkle and verve,

But speak without reservations of their Anglo-Saxon reserve.

After listening to little groups of English ladies and
gentlemen at cocktail parties and in hotels and

Pullmans, of defining Anglo-Saxon reserve I despair,

But I think it consists of assuming that nobody else is there,

And I shudder to think where Anglo-Saxon reserve ends when I consider where it begins,

Which is in a few high-pitched statements of what one's income is and just what foods give one a rash and whether one and one's husband or wife sleep in a double bed or twins.

All good young Englishmen go to Oxford or Cambridge and they all write and publish books before their graduation,

And I often wondered how they did it until I realized that they have to do it because their genteel accents are so developed that they can no longer understand each other's spoken words so the written word is their only means of intercommunication.

England is the last home of the aristocracy, and the art of protecting the aristocracy from the encroachments of commerce has been raised to quite an art,

Because in America a rich butter-and-egg man is only a rich butter-and-egg man or at most an honorary LL.D. of some hungry university, but in England why before he knows it he is Sir Benjamin Buttery, Bart.

Anyhow, I think the English people are sweet,

And we might as well get used to them because when they slip and fall they always land on their own or somebody else's feet.

WAITING FOR THE BIRDIE

Some hate broccoli, some hate bacon,
I hate having my picture taken.
How can your family claim to love you
And then demand a picture of you?
The electric chair is a comfortable chair,
But I know an equally comfortless pair;
One is the dentist's, my good sirs,
And the other is the photographer's.
Oh, the fly in all domestic ointments
Is affectionate people who make appointments
To have your teeth filled left and right,
Or your face reproduced in black and white.
You open the door and you enter the studio,
And you feel less cheerio than nudio.
The hard light shines like seventy suns,
And you know that your features are foolish ones.
The photographer says, Natural, please,
And you cross your knees and uncross your knees
Like a duke in a high society chronicle
The camera glares at you through its monocle
And you feel ashamed of your best attire,
Your nose itches, your palms perspire,
Your muscles stiffen, and all the while
You smile and smile and smile and smile.
It's over; you weakly grope for the door;
It's not; the photographer wants one more.
And if this experience you survive,
Wait, just wait till the proofs arrive.

You look like a drawing by Thurber or Bab,
Or a gangster stretched on a marble slab.
And all your dear ones, including your wife,
Say There he is, that's him to the life!
Some hate broccoli, some hate bacon,
But I hate having my picture taken.

THIS WAS TOLD ME IN CONFIDENCE

Oh, I do like a little bit of gossip
In the course of a cozy little chat,
And I often wonder why
My neighbors all imply
I'm a pussy, I'm a tabby, I'm a cat.
Mrs. Dooley murmured meow at me this morning;
Mrs. Cohen would have cut me if she could;
But my feelings aren't so filmy
That names are going to kill me,
And a little bit of gossip does me good.

Oh, I do like a little bit of gossip;
I am pleased with Mr. Moffet's double life.
It's provocative to watch
Mr. Taylor guzzle Scotch;
I wonder if he knows about his wife?
The sheriff wants a word with Mrs. Walker;
She doesn't pay her bills the way she should;
Yet I hear from several sources
That she gambles on the horses —
Oh, a little bit of gossip does me good.

Oh, I do like a little bit of gossip;
It seems to lend a savor to my tea;
The deplorable mistakes
That everybody makes
Are calories and vitamins to me.
If I tell you Mrs. Drew is off to Reno,
You are not to breathe a word, that's understood;

For I said to Mrs. Drew
That I heard it all from you —
Oh, a little bit of gossip does me good.

Oh, I do like a little bit of gossip,
But for scandal or for spite there's no excuse:
To think of Mrs. Page
Telling lies about my age!
Well, her tongue is like her morals, rather loose.
Mrs. Murgatroyd eats opium for breakfast,
And claims I'm running after Mr. Wood;
That sort of vicious slander
Arouses all my dander —
But a little bit of gossip does me good.

RECIPE FOR A DICTATORSHIP

First catch your country,

Which is not so difficult for a demagogue of sufficient
    ruthlessness, plausibility and effrontery,

But if you catch it by war or revolution debilitated,

Your task will be facilitated.

Its neck is what you place your foot upon,

And then you tell it that by every other nation in the
    world it is put upon,

And you wear some kind of childish raw head and
    bloody bones uniform because you wouldn't be a
    dictator if you weren't a good showman,

And you keep repeating that your people are hemmed
    in by a steel ring of predatory foemen,

And as there is really lots of room for everybody in
    your country because there aren't so many people
    in it as there were before the war,

Why, you shout that there aren't enough people to de-
    fend the country from its evil neighbors and you
    command all patriotic citizens to have a lot more,

And you offer prizes for triplets and twins,

And the race begins,

And the birthrate leaps like a startled fawn,

And you urge it on and on and on,

The cry is breed! breed!

Breed with speed!

The big bad enemy is at the gate,

Breed for the state!

So every hut produces its enormous family,

And you go around and pat the children on the head

and the fathers on the back and smile a big smile with your teeth all glistening and enamelly,

And pretty soon you have your country populated as full as the Bronx Express during the rush hour and you say My gracious me!

What a wonderful, progressive, up-and-coming, expanding nation are we!

We'll have to take over somebody else's country because in our own country there isn't room for us,

And everybody in the League of Nations is a rotten egg if they don't say Rah rah siss boom for us!

So then you go out to take over somebody else's nation,

And that takes care of your surplus population,

So then you find you haven't got as many people in your country as your ambitions need,

So you inform your people again that they had better hurry up and breed,

Which maybe they don't and maybe they do,

And again maybe, dear dictator, they begin to cogitate about you.

THE STRANGE CASE OF THE TSAR'S
SUPERIORITY COMPLEX

Once upon a time there was a Balkan state.

✧

The name of the State was Bulgonia.

✧

Bulgonia was ruled by a Tsar.

✧

The name of the Tsar was Borealis.

✧

He was known as Tsar Borealis of Bulgonia because his name was Borealis and he was the Tsar of Bulgonia.

✧

Tsar Borealis was very democratic.

✧

You may think it difficult for a Tsar to be democratic.

✧

It isn't.

✧

If a postman gets a cold, it's unfortunate.

✧

If a Tsar gets a cold, it's democratic.

✧

If a bookkeeper wheels his baby around the block, it's Astoria.

✧

If a Tsar wheels his baby around the block, it's practically Communistic.

✧

If a concierge says he admires American institutions, it's untrue.

∽

If a Tsar says he admires American institutions it's a sign that somebody wants to float a loan.

∽

Tsar Borealis got colds and wheeled his baby around block after block and simply adored American institutions.

∽

He was a one-hundred-per-cent democrat.

∽

When an American is a one-hundred-per-cent democrat he gets in wrong with his wife.

∽

When a Tsar is a one-hundred-per-cent democrat he gets in the papers.

∽

Tsar Borealis's press clippings from New York and Washington alone were practically pushing him out of the palace.

∽

Sofia, so good.

∽

Unfortunately, Tsar Borealis asked his Prime Minister one day what was the source of sleeping sickness.

∽

The Prime Minister told him the tse-tse fly.

∽

Tsar Borealis said the Prime Minister meant the tse fly.

~

The Prime Minister begged His Imperial Highness's
pardon, but said he meant the tse-tse fly.

~

Tsar Borealis wouldn't believe it until he saw it in the
dictionary.

~

Then he was furious.

~

He said democrat or no democrat, he wasn't going to
be out-hyphenated by any African fly.

~

He said that from now on he was the Tsar-tsar Borealis,
and everybody had better look out.

~

The Tsar-Tsar moved at once to Walla Walla.

~

He refused to wear any garment but a lava-lava.

~

I regret to state that it was not long before he perished.

~

But he met the end smiling.

~

The ailment was beri-beri.

DEAR GODMOTHER; I HOPE SHE
BRUISES EASY!

Good morrow, my little man, do you know who I am?
    I am your fairy godmother, that's who,
And can I fix you up with anything you want? Well,
    can a duck swim, and can a cow moo?
Yes, little man, just one wave of my good old wand,
And you shall have anything of which you are fond.
Is it glass slippers you desire, or a cloak of darkness, or
    three wishes, or seven-league boots?
The minute my little man says the word, why the works
    are what godmother shoots.
Perhaps you would prefer
To be a delightful engaging witty raconteur,
So I shall give you the power of remembering all the
    comical anecdotes you hear,
Instead of having them go in one and out the other
    ear.
Is your employment beginning to pall?
Very well, you shall have the choice either of enjoying
    your work or else not having to work at all.
Do you long to excel in repartee, do you yearn for a
    little more dignity and a little less paunch?
Godson, I hereby give you carte blanche.
You shall always hold the major suits and your oppo·
    nents the minors,
And you shall be able to drink the coffee that con·
    fronts you on diners;
In the race to beat the traffic light you shall trounce
    whoever you race with,

And when you stay at hotels you shall find that the
bathrooms are actually supplied with washcloths
to wash your face with;
Your ship shall be constantly coming into harbor,
And you shall know how to talk to a barber;
Your taxes shall be infinitesimal,
And the Department of Internal Revenue shall say you
need never pay a tax again because your return
is a masterpiece right down to the last decimal;
When head waiters attempt to seat you under the electric fan by the service door you shall know how
to quash them with a snub that rankles,
And when you skate you shall skate on your skates in-
stead of on your ankles;
Your children shall not be acrobats and their I.Q.'s
shall be plus and their behavior problems minus;
And you shall be able to step into a ready-made suit
and it shall look as if it had been especially tailored
for you by a tailor who tailors By Appointment to
His Royal Highnus;
And hark ye, godson, I save the best for the last, for lo
and behold!
You shall never catch cold.
Oh, and P.S., godson, just two more words before
Godmother disappears, but Godmother has an
idea they may knock you for a gool:
April Fool!

There are several things in life that keep me guessing,

And one of them is what are the French words for French leave and French fried potatoes and French dressing,

And I am also a trifle vague

About how you ask people to a Dutch treat or talk to them like a Dutch uncle in The Hague.

And why do restaurants put signs in their windows advertising REAL HOME COOKING and expect the customers to come rushing in all panting and overjoyed

When the reason that half the people who eat in restaurants are eating in restaurants is because with home cooking they have become cloyed?

And when is a violin a fiddle?

And when the tide goes out here does it go in somewhere else or does it just pile up and make the ocean deeper in the middle?

And who is the brownie whose duty it is to see that the theater curtain never goes up on time except the one evening that you are late?

And who is the railroad dispatcher who arranges his dispatching so that every time you are about to see something interesting out of your train window your view is cut off by a hundred-car freight?

All these moot questions and many others equally moot if not even mooter

Must be faced by every thinking male and female prac-

tically as soon as they graduate from their kiddie-
kar or scooter,
Because they are the kind of riddles and conundrums
with which life
Is far too too rife,
But fortunately for the human race thinking people
eventually discover that there is only one satisfac-
tory way of dealing with a riddle or a conundrum.
And that is to stop worrying about the answers and just
get clean out from undrum.

Oh, early every afternoon
I like a temporary swoon.
I do not overeat at luncheon,
I do not broach the bowl or puncheon;
Yet the hour from two to three
Is always sleepy-time to me.

Bolt upright at my desk I sit,
My elbows digging into it,
My chin into my hands doth fit,
My careful fingers screen my eyes,
And all my work before me lies,
Which leads inquisitive passer-bys
Who glance my way and see me nod,
To think me wide awake, if odd.

I would not sell my daily swoon
For all the rubies in Rangoon.
What! sell my swoon? My lovely swoon?
Oh, many and many's the afternoon
I've scoured the woods with Daniel Boone,
And sipped a julep with Lorna Doone
And Former Governor Ruby Laffoon.
I'll sell my soul before my swoon,
It's not for sale, my swoon's immune.

From two to three each afternoon
Mine are the Mountains of the moon,
Mine a congenital silver spoon.
And I can lead a lost platoon

Or dive for pearls in a haunted lagoon,
Or guide a stratosphere balloon.
Oh, where the schooner schoons, I schoon,
I can talk lion, or baboon,
Or make a crooner cease to croon.
I like to swoon, for when I swoon
The universe is my macaroon.
Then blessings on thee, my afternoon torpor,
Thou makest a prince of a mental porpor.

THE CITY

This beautiful ditty
Is, for a change, about the city,
Although ditties aren't very popular
Unless they're rural and not metropular.

Sentimentalists object to towns initially
Because they are made artificially,
But so is vaccination,
While smallpox is an original creation.

Artists speak of everything urban
As the W.C.T.U. speaks of rye and bourbon,
And they say cities are only commercial marts,
But they fail to realize that no marts, no arts.

The country was made first,
Yes, but people lived in it and rehearsed,
And when they finally got civilization down,
Why, they moved to town.

City people always want the most faucets
And the comfortablest caucets,
And labor-saving devices in their kitchenette,
And at the movies, armchairs in which to set.

Take country people, they suffer stoically,
But city people prefer to live unheroically;
Therefore city dentistry is less painful,
Because city dentists find it more gainful.

City people are querulous and queasy,
And they'd rather die than not live easy
And if they did die, they'd find fault
If they weren't put in an air-conditioned vault.

Yes, indeed, they are certainly sissies,
Not at all like Hercules or Ulysses,
But because they are so soft,
City life is comfortable, if not perpetually, at least oft.

I don't know exactly how long ago Hector was a pup,
But it was quite long ago, and even then people used
    to have to start their day by getting up.
Yes, people have been getting up for centuries,
They have been getting up in palaces and Pullmans
    and penitentiaries.
One fact for which every historian vouches,
Is that every morning in history began with people get-
    ting up off their couches.
The caveman had to get up before he could go out
    and track the brontosaurus,
Verdi had to get up before he could sit down and com-
    pose the Anvil Chorus,
Alexander had to get up before he could go around be-
    ing dominant,
Even Rip Van Winkle had to get up from one sleep
    before he could climb the mountain and encounter
    the sleep which has made him prominent.
Some get up energetically and some in lassitude's
    throes,
And I myself happen to love a lassitude, a bonnie bon-
    nie lassitude, but be that as it may, however they
    rose, they rose.
Well, birds are descended from birds and flowers are
    descended from flowers,
And human beings are descended from generation after
    generation of ancestors who got up at least once
    every twenty-four hours,
And because birds are descended from birds they don't

have to be forced to sing like birds, instead of squeaking like rats,

And because flowers are descended from flowers they don't have to be forced to smell like flowers, instead of like burning rubber or the Jersey flats,

But you take human beings, why their countless generations of ancestors who were always arising might just as well have spent all their lives on their mattresses or pallets,

Because their descendants haven't inherited any talent for getting up at all, no, every morning they have to be forced to get up either by their own conscience or somebody else's, or alarm clocks or valets.

Well, there is one obvious conclusion that I have always held to,

Which is that if Nature had really intended human beings to get up, why they would get up naturally and wouldn't have to be compelled to.

Winter comes but once a year,
And when it comes it brings the doctor good cheer;
Yes, it comes but once a year but it lasts for most of it,
And you may think there is a chance it may be a mild
    one, but there isn't a ghost of it.
Winter is indeed a season that I would like to apply
    an uncomplimentary name to,
But I really don't mind it as much as the people who
    enjoy it, or at least claim to.
Yes, some people still say ice is nicer than slush,
And to those people I say Hush.
Some people still say snow is nicer than rain,
Which is like being still unreconciled to the defeat of
    James G. Blaine.
Some people still say a freeze is nicer than a thaw,
And I hope they find cold storage Japanese beetles in
    their slaw.

Slush is much nicer than ice because when you step in it
    you simply go splash, instead of immediately de-
    positing either your posterior or your pate on it,
And also you don't have to skate on it.
Rain is much nicer than snow because you don't have
    to have rain plows piling rain up in six-foot piles
    exactly where you want to go,
And you don't have to build rain-men for the kiddies
    and frolic in sleighs and sleds, and also rain is nicer
    because it melts the snow.
A thaw is obviously much nicer than a freeze,

Because it annoys people with skis.

And in all my life I have only known one man who honestly liked winter better than summer,

Because every summer he used to have either his tonsils or his appendix or something out, and every winter he was a plumber.

THE STRANGE CASE OF THE DEAD DIVORCEE

Once upon a time there was a beautiful woman named
Mrs. Geraldine McGregor Hamilton Garfinkle
Boyce.

❧

Her first husband, Mr. McGregor, divorced her for infidelity.

❧

That wasn't his real reason, but he didn't want to blast
her reputation.

❧

Her second husband, Mr. Hamilton, divorced her for
infidelity, too.

❧

He had better grounds, which he was too chivalrous to
mention.

❧

Her third husband, Mr. Garfinkle, was a cad.

❧

He prepared a statement for the press setting forth his
actual motives for divorcing her.

❧

Her white-haired old mother pled tearfully with him
for seven hours, pausing only to telephone her
maid to bring over a dozen clean handkerchiefs.

❧

Mr. Garfinkle, if a cad, was a soft-hearted cad.

❧

He destroyed his original damaging statement and in
formed the press that he was divorcing his wife
for infidelity.

∾

It was in June that Mrs. Geraldine McGregor Hamilton Garfinkle became Mrs. Geraldine McGregor
Hamilton Garfinkle Boyce.

∾

It was in July that Mr. Boyce slaughtered her with a
priceless heirloom, an ice-pick.

∾

At the trial, Mr. Boyce pled guilty.

∾

She was infidelitous, said Mr. Boyce, and I saw red.

∾

Mr. Boyce's lawyer asked him if he didn't have a better
excuse.

∾

Maybe I have, said Mr. Boyce, but my lips are sealed.

∾

De mortuis, you know, said Mr. Boyce.

∾

I will only say that she was infidelitous.

∾

Mr. Boyce was convicted and condemned to die.

∾

Came Mr. Boyce's Execution Eve.

∾

The reporters were already strapping their cameras to
their ankles when a delegation waited upon the
Governor.

The delegation consisted of Mr. McGregor, Mr. Hamilton and Mr. Garfinkle.

∽

There are extenuating circumstances in the case of Mr. Boyce, said Mr. McGregor.

∽

It is time the truth about Geraldine McGregor Hamilton Garfinkle Boyce were told, said Mr. Hamilton.

∽

I would have told it long ago but for my soft heart, said Mr. Garfinkle.

∽

Geraldine McGregor Hamilton Garfinkle Boyce was a juleper-in-the-manger, said Mr. McGregor, Mr. Hamilton and Mr. Garfinkle.

∽

She never drank but half a mint julep, they said.

∽

But when she was offered a mint julep, did she quietly drink half of it and quietly give the other half to her husband when he had finished his?

∽

Not Geraldine McGregor Hamilton Garfinkle Boyce! they said.

∽

She said no thank you, I only want half of one, I'll drink half of my husband's, they said.

∽

Other women's husbands get a julep and a half, they said.

∽

Geraldine McGregor Hamilton Garfinkle Boyce's husbands get half a julep, they said.

∽

The Governor pardoned Mr. Boyce forthwith.

∽

Ten minutes later the Governor's butler discovered the body of the Governor's lady on the veranda.

∽

The ice-pick that protruded from her heart was a priceless heirloom.

EVERYBODY EATS TOO MUCH ANYHOW

You *gulp* your breakfast and glance at the clock,
Through eleventh hour packing you gallop amok
You bundle your bags in the back of the car,
You enter, she enters, and there you are.
You clutch the wheel, she clutches the maps,
And longs for a couple of extra laps.
It's au revoir to your modest abode,
You're gipsies, away on the open road;
Into the highway you burst like a comet or
Heat waves climbing a Kansas thermometer.
The conversation is sweet as clover,
With breakfast practically hardly over.
"Darling, light me a cigarette?"
"At once and with all my heart, my pet;
"And by the way, we are off the track;
"We should have turned left a half-mile back."
You swing around with a cheery smile,
Thus far, a mile is only a mile.
The road is romance, so let it wind,
With breakfast an hour or so behind.
Under the tires the pebbles crunch,
And through the dust creep thoughts of lunch
The speedometer sits on a steady fifty
And more and more does lunch seem nifty.
Your eyes to the road ahead are glued,
She glances about in search of food.
She sees a place. She would like to try it.
She says so. Well, you're already by it.
Ignoring the road, you spot an eatery;

The look of it makes her interior teetery.
She sees a beauty. You're past it again.
Her eyebrows look like ten past ten;
She's simmering now, and so are you,
And your brows register ten to two.
She snubs the excuse as you begin it:
That there'll be another one any minute,
She says there won't. It must be a plot;
She's absolutely correct. There's not.
You finally find one. You stop and alight.
You're both too annoyed to eat a bite.
Oh, this is the gist of my gipsy song:
Next time carry your lunch along.

YES AND NO

Oh would I were a politician,
Or else a person with a mission.
Heavens, how happy I could be
If only I were sure of me.

How would I strut, could I believe
That, out of all the sons of Eve,
God had granted this former youth
A binding option on His truth.

One side of the moon we've seen alone;
The other she has never shown.
What dreamless sleep, what sound digestion,
Were it the same with every question!

Sometimes with secret pride I sigh
To think how tolerant am I;
Then wonder which is really mine:
Tolerance, or a rubber spine?

Once upon a time there was an Italian,
And some people thought he was a rapscallion,
But he wasn't offended,
Because other people thought he was splendid,
And he said the world was round,
And everybody made an uncomplimentary sound,
But his only reply was Pooh,
He replied, Isn't this fourteen ninety-two?
It's time for me to discover America if I know my
    chronology,
And if I discover America you owe me an apology,
So he went and tried to borrow some money from
    Ferdinand
But Ferdinand said America was a bird in the bush
    and he'd rather have a berdinand,
But Columbus' brain was fertile, it wasn't arid,
And he remembered that Ferdinand was married,
And he thought, there is no wife like a misunderstood
    one,
Because her husband thinks something is a terrible
    idea she is bound to think it a good one,
So he perfumed his handkerchief with bay rum and
    citronella,
And he went to see Isabella,
And he looked wonderful but he had never felt sillier,
And she said, I can't place the face but the aroma is
    familiar,
And Columbus didn't say a word,

All he said was, I am Columbus, the fifteenth-century
    Admiral Byrd,

And just as he thought, her disposition was very mal-
    leable,

And she said, Here are my jewels, and she wasn't pe-
    nurious like Cornelia the mother of the Gracchi,
    she wasn't referring to her children, no, she was
    referring to her jewels, which were very very valu-
    able,

So Columbus said, somebody show me the sunset and
    somebody did and he set sail for it,

And he discovered America and they put him in jail
    for it,

And the fetters gave him welts,

And they named America after somebody else,

So the sad fate of Columbus ought to be pointed out
    to every child and every voter,

Because it has a very important moral, which is, Don't
    be a discoverer, be a promoter.

Sometimes it's difficult, isn't it, not to grow grim and
    rancorous
Because man's fate is so counter-clockwise and can-
    tankerous.
Look at all the noble projects that die a-borning,
Look how hard it is to get to sleep at night and then
    how hard it is to wake up in the morning!
Look how when people look at a girl in cold blood they
    can see that she is bow-legged or cross-eyed or
    thinks she is so wonderful or nags or chatters,
And then look how they don't notice it at all when
    they are in love with her which is the critical time
    when it really matters.
How easy to be unselfish in the big things that never
    come up and how hard in the little things that
    come up daily and hourly, oh yes,
Such as what heroic pleasure to give up the last seat
    in a lifeboat to a mother and babe, and what an
    irritation to give some dowdy housewife your seat
    on the Lexington Avenue Express!
How easy for those who do not bulge
To not overindulge!
O universe perverse, why and whence your perverse-
    ness?
Why do you not teem with betterness instead of worse-
    ness?
Why is it your gospel
To go around making everything just as complicated
    as pospel?

Do you get your only enjoyment
Out of humanity's annoyment?
Because a point I would like to discuss
Is, why wouldn't it be just as easy for you to make
   things easy for us?
But no, you will not listen, expostulation is useless,
Home is the fisherman empty-handed, home is the
   hunter caribouless and mooseless.
Humanity must continue to follow the sun around
And accept the eternal run-around.
Well, and if that be the case, why come on humanity!
So long as it is our fate to be irked all our life let us
   just keep our heads up and take our irking with
   insouciant urbanity.

ONE MAN'S MEED IS ANOTHER MAN'S OVEREMPHASIS

I salute the section of our lordly Sunday journals which
is entitled Scores of College Football Games Con-
tinued from Page One,

Because there a flock of not very notorious institutions
of learning find their annual place in the sun.

Yes, the football season is a kindly time of year,

And during it we read of campuses of which at other
times we do not often hear.

Would a playwright, for instance, ordinarily select Aurora as the Alma Mater for his hero?

Yet it is here recorded that Aurora one week held
Wright Jr. to a six-to-six tie and the next
week took the measure of Wartburg, nineteen to
zero.

Yes, and the St. Cloud Teachers are an aggregation
that no college-lover can conscientiously shelve,

Because they nosed out the Bemidji Teachers thirteen
to twelve.

Oh ye of little faith who take Yale and Notre Dame
for your Alpha and Omega,

What about Hiwassee, which outscored Biltmore, and
Dillard, which engaged in a Homeric deadlock
with Talladega?

When better endowments are offered,

Well, what's the matter with Augustana and Millsaps
and Spearfish and Gustavus Adolphus and Wof-
ford?

So if anybody makes derogatory remarks about the football season let us answer with scornful defiance,
And meanwhile let us not forget that Huron beat Yankton six to nothing on the very same day that Jamestown smothered Wahpeton Science.

THE STRANGE CASE OF THE PLEASING
TAXI-DRIVER

Once upon a time there was a taxi-driver named Llewellyn Abdullah — White — Male — 5–10 1/2 — 170.

～

Llewellyn had promised his mother he would be the best taxi-driver in the world.

～

His mother was in Heaven.

～

At least, she was in a Fool's Paradise because her boy was the best taxi-driver in the world.

～

He was, too.

～

He called his male passengers Sir instead of Mac, and his female passengers Madam instead of Sister.

～

On rainy nights his flag was always up.

～

He knew not only how to find the Waldorf, but the shortest route to 5954 Gorsuch Avenue.

～

He said Thank you when tipped, and always had change for five dollars.

～

He never drove with a cigar in his mouth, lighted or unlighted.

If you asked him to please not drive so fast, he drove not so fast, and didn't get mad about it, either.

~

He simply adored traffic cops, and he was polite to Sunday drivers.

~

When he drove a couple through the park he never looked back and he never eavesdropped.

~

My boy is the best taxi-driver in the world and no eavesdropper, said his mother.

~

The only trouble was that the bad taxi-drivers got all the business.

~

Llewellyn shrank from White — Male — 5–10 1/2 — 170 to Sallow — Male — 5–9 3/4 — 135.

~

Cheest, Llewellyn, said his mother.

~

Cheest, Mother, replied Llewellyn.

~

Llewellyn and his mother understood each other.

~

He took his last five dollars in dimes and nickles which he had been saving for change and spent it on cigars at two for a nickel.

~

The next day he insulted seven passengers and a traffic
cop, tore the fender off a car from Enid, Okla-
homa, and passed through 125th Street while taking a dear old lady from 52nd to 58th.

ⱺ

That evening he had forty dollars on the clock.

ⱺ

Llewellyn is no longer the best taxi-driver in the world,
but his license reads White — Male — 5–11 — 235.

ⱺ

In the park he is the father of all eavesdroppers.

ⱺ

Couples who protest find him adamant.

ⱺ

Since he is the father of all eavesdroppers and adamant,
I think we might call him an Adam-ant-Eves-
dropper and there leave him.

ⱺ

Good-by, Llewellyn.

Poets aren't very useful,
Because they aren't very consumeful or very produceful.
Even poets of great promise
Don't contribute much to trade and commerce,
To which, indeed, even poets of great achievement
Are a positive bereavement,
Because they aren't very sensible,
Because they think buying and selling are cheap and
     lousy and reprehensible,
And this is a topic about which poets are people to
     whom you cannot tell anything,
Because they are people who cannot afford to buy any·
     thing and are seldom glib enough to sell anything,
So there is some excuse for the way they feel,
Because they have seen lots of sunsets but no big deals
     so it follows naturally that they consider a sunset
     more important than a big deal.
Some poets are bitter,
But they are preferable to the poets who are all of a
     twitter,
But even the poets who are all of a twitter are as de·
     pendable as Rotary
Compared to what each of them has around him which
     is a rapturous coterie,
Because every poet is threatened constantly by one dis-
     aster,
Which is that a lot of otherwise thwarted male and
     female ladies will go around calling him Master,
And then there is nothing to do but surrender,

And then it is good-by old poetry, hello old theosophy
and gender,

And yet on the other hand if a poet isn't fed by a lot
of male and female ladies who are affected,

Why, until long after he is dead or gets the Pulitzer
Prize, why he is neglected.

But the worst thing that can happen to a poet

Is to be ashamed of poetry as poetry so that he ex-
cuses himself for writing it by writing it sociologi-
cally in terms of Moscow or Detroet,

Which is something I regret,

Because it is like a preacher taking a couple of high-
balls and telling a dirty story just to prove that he
is a hail fellow well met,

So my advice to mothers is if you are the mother of a
poet don't gamble on the chance that future generations may crown him.

Follow your original impulse and drown him.

Does anybody mind if I don't live in a house that is
    quaint?

Because, for one thing, quaint houses are generally
    houses where plumbing ain't,

And while I don't hold with fanatical steel-and-glass
    modernistic bigots,

Still, I do think that it simplifies life if you live it sur-
    rounded by efficient pipes and faucets and spig-
    gots.

I admit that wells and pumps and old oaken buckets
    are very nice in a poem or ode,

But I feel that in literature is where they should have
    their permanent abode,

Because suppose you want a bath,

It is pleasanter to be able to take it without leaving a
    comfortable stuffy room and going out into the
    bracing fresh air and bringing back some water
    from the end of a path.

Another thing about which I am very earnest,

Is that I do like a house to be properly furnaced,

Because if I am out in the bracing fresh air I expect to
    be frozen,

But to be frigid in a stuffy room isn't what I would have
    chosen.

And when you go to bed in a quaint house the whole
    house grumbles and mutters,

And you are sure the walls will be shattered by clatter-
    ing shutters.

At least you hope it's the shutters but you fear it's a

gang of quaint ghosts warming up for twelve
o'clock,

And you would lock yourself snugly in but the quaint
old key won't turn in the quaint old lock,

So you would pull the bedclothes snugly up over your
head and lie there till a year from next autumn,

Were it not a peculiarity of bedclothes in quaint houses
that if you pull them up on top, why your feet
stick out at the bautum,

But anyhow you find a valley among the hilltops of
your mattress and after a while slumber comes
softly stealing,

And that is when you feel a kiss on your cheek and you
think maybe it is a goodnight kiss from your guard-
ian angel, but it isn't, it's a leak in the ceiling.

Oh, I yield to none in my admiration of the hardy
colonists and their hardy spouses,

But I still feel that their decadent descendants build
more comfortable houses.

ALLERGY MET A BEAR

I heard them speak of allergy,
I asked them to explain,
Which when they did, I asked them
To please explain again.

I found the pith of allergy
In Bromides tried and true;
For instance, you like lobster,
But lobster don't like you.

Does aspirin cause your eyes to cross?
Do rose-leaves make you nervy?
Do old canaries give you boils?
Do kittens give you scurvy?

Whatever turns your skin to scum,
Or turns your blood to glue,
Why, that's the what, the special what,
That you're allergic to.

O allergy, sweet allergy,
Thou lovely word to me!
Swift as an heiress Reno-bound
I called on my M.D.

This doctor was obliged to me
For reasons I must edit.
(I knew he had two extra wives,
And neither did him credit.)

I spoke to him of allergy;
Perhaps I clenched my fist;
But when I left his domicile
I had a little list.

I can't attend the opera now,
Or sleep within a tent;
I cannot ride in rumble seats;
My allergies prevent.

Oh, garden parties speed my pulse
And pound my frame to bits;
I'd mind the child on Thursdays,
But children give me fits.

When Duty sounds her battlecry,
Say never that I shirk;
It isn't laziness at all,
But an allergy to work.

Women still excel as mothers,
Women still excel as wives,
Women still, in spite of diets,
Lead with forks and knives.
Women have the fairest faces,
Women have the softest hearts,
Women gain the greenest laurels
When they woo the arts.
Let me add to this preamble,
Women, women shouldn't gamble.

Yip! Whoop! Boop-boop-a-doop!
The frenzied treble rises,
The welkin reels to soprano squeals
When ladies win the prizes.
Fret! Fume! Grim, glum gloom!
Oh, what a crooked bank!
Clear the path for righteous wrath
When the ladies draw a blank.
Oh, girls will gamble if they choose,
But they shouldn't win and they shouldn't lose.

Woman! First in intuition!
Lovely woman! Still untaught
That every time somebody wins,
Someone else is caught.
Woman! Hers the sweetest accent
Heard on this terrestrial stage —
But not when raised in yelps of triumph,
Not when hoarse with rage.

That woman most is worth escorting
Who never, never goes a-sporting.

Bliss! Joy! Boy, oh boy!
She won through personal merit;
The tip came through, the dream came true,
The rabbit bit the ferret.
Boo! Shame! the world's to blame!
The cards were stacked agin her!
Rise, Huey, rise, some game devise
With every lady a winner.
Nevertheless, the girl I choose
Will never win and never lose.

MIDSUMMER'S DAYMARE

Mumbo jumbo, what have we here?
Why we have the longest day in the year.
This is the rarest day of June,
And it's weeks and weeks from dawn to noon.
This is the calendar's blazing highlight,
It's months and months from noon to twilight.
Lucky are they who retain their friends
Through the day that seldom if ever ends.
Take a modest date, like December twenty,
And still the telephone jangles plenty,
Still you encounter bores enough,
Obligations and chores enough,
Visitors to avoid enough
Like something out of Freud enough,
Creditors, editors, tears and combats,
Newsreel beauties embracing wombats,
Feeble coffee and vanishing waiters,
Newsreel girls riding alligators,
Traffic and taxes and dues and duties
And candidates kissing newsreel beauties.
Oh, man has need of all his strength
To survive a day of medium length;
What wonder, then, that man grows bitter
On a day that sits like a flagpole-sitter?
Mumbo jumbo, noon infernal,
This, my dears, is the day eternal.
You toil for a dollar or two per diem,
You mope and hope for the blessed P.M.,
You look at the clock, you're ready for mayhem;

Is it P.M. yet? No, it's still the A.M.!
On farm and field, in office and park,
This is the day that won't get dark.
Dusk is an exile, night has fled,
Never again shall we get to bed,
The sun has swallowed the moon and stars,
Midnight lies with the buried Czars.
This is the guerdon of prayer and fasting:
Glorious day, day everlasting!

Once upon a time there was a young man named Harold Scrutiny.

ண

Harold had many virtues and practically no vices.

ண

He smoked, to be sure.

ண

Also he drank and swore.

ண

Moreover, he was a pickpocket.

ண

But, for all that, Harold was no prude.

ண

I am no prude, Harold often said.

ண

But Detective Guilfoyle of the Pickpocket Squad is a prude, the old prude, said Harold.

ண

One day Harold went into the subway to pick some pockets.

ண

There was a man on the platform penciling a beard on the lady on the toothpaste placard.

ண

Hey, said Harold.

ண

Hey who, said the man.

ண

Hey you, that's hey who, said Harold.

~

Aren't you going to give her a moustache?

~

Sure I'm going to give her a moustache, said the man.

~

What do you think I am?

~

I think you're somebody that puts the beard on ladies
   on toothpaste placards before they put on the
   moustache, said Harold.

~

Don't you know enough to put the moustache on first?

~

You put the moustache on first, why then you can turn
   it up or turn it down, whichever you want, said
   Harold.

~

You try to turn a moustache down after the beard's on,
   it runs into the beard, said Harold.

~

It don't look like a moustache, only like a beard grows
   up and down both.

~

Go on, said the man, go on and pick some pockets.

~

Harold turned to his work, but his mind was elsewhere.

~

Suddenly the lady on the toothpaste placard got off
   the toothpaste placard and arrested him.

~

It was Detective Guilfoyle of the Pickpocket Squad all the time.

∽

You got a beard grows up and down both, said Harold.

∽

Detective Guilfoyle searched Harold.

∽

He certainly was surprised at what he found.

∽

So was Harold.

∽

Harold hadn't picked any pockets at all because his mind was elsewhere.

∽

He had picked a peck of pickled peppers.

∽

Detective Guilfoyle wanted to call Harold a name, but he couldn't because he was a prude.

∽

Harold picked his pocket and later became the smok-ingest swearingest, drinkingest Assistant District Attorney the county ever had.

∽

Don't be a prude.

Cows go around saying Moo,
But the wind goes around saying Woooo.
Ghosts say Woooo to you, too,
And sometimes they say Boo to you, too,
But everybody has heard the wind and few people have
    heard a ghost,
So it is commonly supposed that the wind says Woooo
    the most.
Scientists try to tell us that wind is caused by at-
    mospheric conditions at the North Pole or over
    distant Canadian ranches,
But I guess scientists don't ever get to the country be-
    cause everybody who has ever been in the country
    knows that wind is caused by the trees waggling
    their branches.
On the ocean, where there are no trees, they refer to
    the wind as gales,
And it is probably caused by whales,
And in the Sahara, where there are no trees or whales
    either, they call the wind a simoom or some-
    thing,
And it is the result of the profanation of Tutankha-
    men's tomb or something,
But anyhow wherever you are, the wind is always nigh
    and I for one hope it won't come any nigher,
Because it makes cold colder and heat hotter and rain
    wetter and dust drier,
And it can cover a lot of time in a very short space,

And it doesn't matter whether it's an East Wind and you are heading West or a North Wind and you are heading South, it always manages to be right in your face.

Ill winds blow nobody good and they also blow new hats into mud puddles and voracious clouds of mosquitoes into propinquity with your hide,

And they make your cigarette burn down on just one side.

Some people are very refined,

And when they recite poetry or sing songs they pronounce wind, wined.

Well, dear wined, every time you say Wooooo,

Why I wish you would say it to people who say wined, right after you have said it somewhere where somebody is making fertilizer or glue.

There are some people of whom I would certainly like
 to be one,
Who are the people who get things done.
They never forget to send their evening shirts to the
 laundry and then when they need them can't find
 anything but a lot of shirts without any starch,
And they always file their income tax return by the
 fourteenth of March.
They balance their checkbooks every month and their
 figures always agree with the bank's,
And they are prompt in writing letters of condolence
 or thanks.
They never leave anything to chance,
But always make reservations in advance.
When they get out of bed they never neglect to don
 slippers so they never pick up athlete's foot or a
 cold or a splinter,
And they hang their clothes up on hangers every night
 and put their winter clothes away every summer
 and their summer clothes away every winter.
Before spending any money they insist on getting an
 estimate or a sample,
And if they lose anything from a shoelace to a diamond
 ring it is covered by insurance more than ample.
They have budgets and what is more they live inside
 of them,
Even though it means eating things made by recipes
 clipped from the Sunday paper that you'd think
 they would have died of them.

They serve on committees

And improve their cities.

They are modern knight errants

Who remember their godchildren's birthdays and the
    anniversaries of their godchildrens' parents,

And in cold weather they remember the birds and sup-
    ply them with sunflower seed and suet,

And whatever they decide to do, whether it's to save
    twenty-five per cent of their salary or learn Italian
    or write a musical comedy or touch their toes a
    hundred times every morning before breakfast, why
    they go ahead and do it.

People who get things done lead contented lives, or at
    least I guess so,

And I certainly wish that either I were more like them
    or they were less so.

SPRING SONG

Listen, buds, it's March twenty-first;
Don't you know enough to burst?
Come on, birds, unlock your throats!
Come on, gardeners, shed your coats!
Come on zephyrs, come on flowers,
Come on grass, and violet showers!
And come on, lambs, in frisking flocks!
Salute the vernal equinox!
Twang the cheerful lute and zither!
Spring is absolutely hither!
Yester eve was dark despair,
With winter, winter, everywhere;
Today, upon the other hand,
'Tis spring throughout this happy land.
Oh, such is Nature's chiaroscuro,
According to the Weather Bureau.

Then giddy-ap, Napoleon! Giddy-ap, Gideon!
The sun has crossed the right meridian!
What though the blasts of Winter sting?
Officially, at least, it's Spring,
And be it far from our desire
To make the Weather Man a liar!

So, blossom, ye parks, with cozy benches,
Occupied by blushing wenches!
Pipe, ye frogs, while swains are sighing,
And furnaces unwept are dying!
Crow, ye cocks, a little bit louder!

Mount, ye sales of paint and powder!
Croon, ye crooner, yet more croonishly!
Shine, ye moon, a lot more moonishly!
And oh ye brooklets, burst your channels!
And oh ye camphor, greet ye flannels!
And bloom, ye clothesline, bloom with wash,
Where erstwhile squudged the grim galosh!
Ye transit lines, abet our follies
By turning loose your open trolleys!
And ye, ye waking hibernators,
Drain anti-freeze from your radiators!
While ye, ye otherwise useless dove,
Remember, please, to rhyme with love.

Then giddy-ap, Napoleon! Giddy-ap, Gideon!
The sun has crossed the right meridian!
What though the blasts of Winter sting?
Officially, at least, it's Spring!

SHRINKING SONG

Woollen socks, woollen socks!
Full of color, full of clocks!
Plain and fancy, yellow, blue,
From the counter beam at you.
O golden fleece, O magic flocks!
O irresistible woollen socks!
O happy haberdasher's clerk
Amid that galaxy to work!
And now it festers, now it rankles
Not to have them round your ankles;
Now with your conscience do you spar;
They look expensive, and they are;
Now conscience whispers, You ought not to,
And human nature roars, You've got to!
Woollen socks, woollen socks!
First you buy them in a box.
You buy them several sizes large,
Fit for Hercules, or a barge.
You buy them thus because you think
These lovely woollen socks may shrink.
At home you don your socks with ease,
You find the heels contain your knees;
You realize with saddened heart
Their toes and yours are far apart.
You take them off and mutter Bosh,
You up and send them to the wash.
Too soon, too soon the socks return,
Too soon the horrid truth you learn;
Your woollen socks can not be worn

Unless a midget child is born,
And either sockless you must go,
Or buy a sock for every toe.
Woollen socks, woollen socks!
Infuriating paradox!
Hosiery wonderful and terrible,
Heaven to wear, and yet unwearable.
The man enmeshed in such a quandary
Can only hie him to the laundry,
And while his socks are hung to dry,
Wear them once as they're shrinking by.

Darling, what is that?
That, angel, is a hat.
Are you positive? Are you certain?
Are you sure it's not a curtain?
Shall you really place your head in it?
How's for keeping cake or bread in it?
Do not wear it on your head;
Find some other use instead.
Say a cloth for drying dishes,
Or a net for catching fishes,
Or a veil by night to veto
The bill of the mosquito?
Darling, what is that?
Are you sure it is a hat?
And if so, what was the matter
With the hatter?
Was he troubled? Was he ill?
Was he laughing fit to kill?
Oh, what was on his mind
As he designed?
Had he gone without his supper?
Was he dressing in an upper?
Did he plot a wily plan
To annoy his fellow man?
Is its aspect, rear and frontal,
Intended to disgruntle,
Or was it accidental
And is he now repental?

Are memoirs of the brim
Now agony to him?
Do visions of the crown
Drag his spirits down?
Oh, may the Furies batter
That eleven-fingered hatter!
May doom and gloom enswaddle
The creator of this model!
I hope he made a lot of them,
That dozens he has got of them;
I hope he has a harem,
And all his spouses warem.

THE STRANGE CASE OF MR. FORTAGUE'S
DISAPPOINTMENT

*Once upon a time there was a man named Mr. Lionel
Fortague.*

✧

He didn't have very much to talk about.

✧

*In summer he used to ask people if it was hot enough
for them.*

✧

It always was.

✧

*In winter he used to ask people if it was cold enough
for them.*

✧

It always was.

✧

*Mr. Lionel Fortague got pretty sick of people it was
hot enough for.*

✧

He got pretty sick of people it was cold enough for, too.

✧

He decided he would arise and go now.

✧

He decided he would go to Innisfree.

✧

*The people of Innisfree are different, thought Mr.
Lionel Fortague.*

✧

As soon as he got to Innisfree he asked the people it it was cold enough for them.

ↄ⅏

They asked him What? Was what cold enough for who?

ↄ⅏

Mr. Lionel Fortague was delighted.

ↄ⅏

I knew Innisfree would be different, he said to himself.

ↄ⅏

He could hardly wait for summer to verify his conclusion.

ↄ⅏

As soon as summer came he asked everybody if it was hot enough for them.

ↄ⅏

Everybody said the question was familiar but they couldn't remember the answer.

ↄ⅏

Mr. Lionel Fortague said he would settle down on Innisfree, the home of iridescent chitchat.

ↄ⅏

He said he would a small cabin build there, of clay and wattles made.

ↄ⅏

Everybody said did he mean he would build a small cabin there, made of clay and wattles?

ↄ⅏

Mr. Lionel Fortague said yes, but his way of putting it was more poetic.

ↄ⅏

Everybody said maybe, but they were all out of wattles.

~

Mr. Lionel Fortague grew very angry at the people of
   Innisfree.

~

He a small cabin built there, of clay and beaverboard
   made.

~

He a fierce-looking dog at an annual clearance sale
   bought, and it the people of Innisfree one by one
   to bite he instructed.

~

My, he was disappointed.

~

He had forgotten that a bargain dog never bites.

Lots of truisms don't have to be repeated but there is
    one that has got to be,

Which is that it is much nicer to be happy than it is
    not to be,

And I shall even add to it by stating unequivocally and
    without restraint

That you are much happier when you are happy than
    when you ain't.

Some people are just naturally Pollyanna,

While others call for sugar and cream and strawberries
    on their manna.

Now, I think we all ought to say a fig for the happiness
    that comes of thinking helpful thoughts and search-
    ing your soul,

The most exciting happiness is the happiness generated
    by forces beyond your control,

Because if you just depend on your helpful thoughts
    for your happiness and would just as soon drink
    buttermilk as champagne, and if mink is no better
    than lapin to you,

Why you don't even deserve to have anything nice and
    exciting happen to you.

If you are really Master of your Fate,

It shouldn't make any difference to you whether Cleo-
    patra or the Bearded Lady is your mate,

So I hold no brief for the kind of happiness or the kind
    of unhappiness that some people constantly carry
    around in their breast,

Because that kind of happiness simply consists of being resigned to the worst just as that kind of unhappiness consists of being resentful of the best.

No, there is only one kind of happiness that I take the stump for,

Which is the kind that comes when something so wonderful falls in your lap that joy is what you jump for,

Something not of your own doing,

When the blue sky opens and out pops a refund from the Government or an invitation to a terrapin dinner or an unhoped for yes from the lovely creature you have been disconsolately wooing.

And obviously such miracles don't happen every day,

But here's hoping they may,

Because then everybody would be happy except the people who pride themselves on creating their own happiness who as soon as they saw everybody who didn't create their own happiness happy they would probably grieve over sharing their own heretofore private sublimity,

A condition which I could face with equanimity.

Everybody knows how the waters come down at Lo
    dore,
But what about voices coming up through the floor?
Oh yes, every time that into a task you set your teeth
Something starts talking in the room underneath,
And no matter how many authorities you quiz,
You can never find out who or what it is;
You know one thing about it and nothing more,
That it is just something that goes around making
    noises that come up through the floor,
And you never get a view of it,
But you deduce that there are at least two of it,
And sometimes it sings the Indian Love Call and some-
    times it sings Lead, Kindly Light, by Cardinal
    Newman,
But even then it doesn't sound human,
And sometimes it just gobbles,
And the sound wibbles and wobbles,
And sometimes it snarls like a ghoul interrupted at its
    unholy feast,
And sometimes it just mutters like blood going down
    the drain of a tub after a murderer has finished
    dismembering the deceased;
It cackles, it crackles, it drones, it buzzes, it chortles,
It utters words but in no tongue spoken by mortals,
Yes, its language is a mystery for evermore,
The language of whatever it is that makes the noise
    that comes up through the floor,
And you shiver and quiver and wonder,

What's under?

Is it banshees or goblins or leprechauns, or trolls or something?

Or pixies or vampires or lost souls or something?

What is it below?

Better not, better not know.

Don't let it upset you,

But also don't overlook the possibility that someday whatever it is that makes the noises that come up through the floor may come up through the floor and get you.

OH, DID YOU GET THE TICKETS? BECAUSE I DON'T THINK I'LL GO, AFTER ALL

Women are more privileged than men, because if a man
    hasn't any muscle he can't be muscular,
But even if a woman hasn't any bustle she can still be
    buscular,
And women have one particular important privilege,
Which is changing their mind, which we shall call
    swivelege,
And I don't know the exact percentage of it,
But I should say that in about ninety-five out of every
    hundred decisions they take advantage of it;
Indeed, just as you might say that if you don't discard
    a green persimmon in favor of a ripe one you are
    making a persimmon error,
Why, women feel that their first decision is simply a
    preliminerror,
But the path by which they arrive at their final de-
    cision is a devious one,
And somehow they never communicate their final de-
    cision to you until you have acted irrevocably on
    their previous one,
Because some women may go so far as to treat some
    men leniently,
But never to the extent of changing their mind help-
    fully if they can change it inconveniently.
Just as it really begins to rain they announce that what
    they would simply adore is gumdrops, and you
    mention the rain, and they give you a look that
    implies that your spine is spaghetti and your soul
    is lard,

So you say you will go get the gumdrops and they
thank you sweetly and say for heaven's sake don't
get the squashy kind, get them good and hard,

So you go out and you have to go to three places before
you can unearth the hard kind, and you return
dripping and hand the box over and they gaze at
you with dreamy eyes as if they had just been
gazing on some angelic vision aloft,

And they say they are so sorry but right after you went
out they remembered that a fortuneteller told
them hard gumdrops were unlucky, would you
mind exchanging these for soft?

And sometimes they get you to go to an auction and
overbid extravagantly for a clock of ormolu,

And if you protest they say " 'Oo doesn't know anysing
about art, 'oo dreat big darlin' subnormal 'oo,"

And an hour later they say, "That clock wasn't the
right shape for the mantelpiece, was it?"

So they ask you to calmly go back and calmly ask the
auctioneer to return your deposit.

Oh, a boy's will is the wind's will, if we are to believe
the poet,

But a girl's will is a won't, but not until it doesn't do
you any good to know it.

FRIDAY COMES AROUND SO QUICKLY

How oft I think I do not wish
Ever again to feed on fish.
Though known as one who seldom belittles
Anything in the shape of victuals,
I find it easy not to crave
These denizens of stream and wave.
Where else does life hold such a letdown
As when you at the table setdown;
You've toiled all day with main and might,
You have a congressman's appetite;
Your palate it would barely tickle
To eat the buffalo off a nickel.
And after that the Indian chief;
But what you really want is beef.
Rich, dripping slabs of roasted kine,
Thick as your thumb and red as wine;
Or maybe a steak that sizzles like sin,
All crisp outside, all juicy within;
You could cope with platters of chops and chickens
Like an eater out of Scott or Dickens;
You don't care what you get to eat
As long as it's meat and still more meat.
The meal is ready, the hands are dealt —
And you catch the eye of a sneering smelt.
Oh, speak to me not of trout or bluefish,
I remain unmoved and coldly aloofish;
Salmon and mackerel tempt me not,
Nor the pompano nor the Norfolk spot;

The pallid cod and the finnan haddie
Merely irk this carnivorous laddie.
Whether captured by net or by baited hook
Fish never lose that fishlike look;
Season away, they never waver,
Never surrender their fishlike flavor.
Fish are relished by other fish,
Sea gulls think them a savory dish,
But I will take them, if taken at all,
Mounted and hung on a barroom wall.

WASHINGTON'S BIRTHDAY EVE

George Washington was a gentleman,
A soldier and a scholar;
He crossed the Delaware with a boat,
The Potomac, with a dollar.
The British faced him full of joy,
And departed full of sorrow;
George Washington was a gentleman.
His birthday is tomorrow.

When approached by fellow patriots,
And asked for his opinion,
He spoke in accents clear and bold,
And, probably, Virginian.
His winter home at Valley Forge
Was underheated, rather.
He possessed a sturdy Roman nose,
And became his country's father.

His army was a hungry horde,
Ill-armed, worse-clad Colonials;
He was our leading President,
And discouraged ceremonials.
His portrait on our postage stamps,
It does him less than justice;
He was much respected by his wife,
The former Mrs. Custis.

He routed George's scarlet coats;
(Though oft by Congress hindered)
When they fortified the leeward side,
He slashed them from the windward.

He built and launched our Ship of State,
He brought it safe to harbor;
He wore no beard upon his chin,
Thanks to his faithful barber.

George Washington was a gentleman,
His birthday is tomorrow.
He filled his country's friends with joy,
His country's foes, with sorrow.
And so my dears, his grateful land
In robes of glory clad him.
George Washington was a gentleman.
I'm glad his parents had him.

I'LL BE UP IN A MINUTE

Oh some men want their vanished youth,
And some a million dollars,
And expensive cars and big cigars,
And shirts with silken collars.
Some wish to paint the beautifulest,
Some wish to paint the oddest;
But never have I aspired so high;
My dream is meek and modest.

It's ten more minutes in bed
With a yaw and a yawn and a yaw,
Yes, ten more minutes in bed,
When the sunlight's bricht and braw;
To swoon like a weeping willow
With a ho and a hum and a ho,
Once more across my pillow,
And to roll from to to fro;
To thwart the meddlesome rising bell
With a blanket o'er my head;
To yawn at the dawn and carry on
For ten more minutes in bed.

Oh sleep at eve is a blessed thing,
And sleep at night is blesseder,
And poets leap to write of sleep,
Death's brother and ambassador.
I welcome sleep at any hour,
I have, since I was born;
But the sleep I love all sleep above
Is a little more sleep at morn.

Oh, ten more minutes in bed,
With a yaw and a yawn and a yaw,
Just ten more minutes in bed,
For aged muscles to thaw.
To stretch like a drowsy feline,
With a ho and a hum and a ho,
To follow a flowery beeline
To the land where the good dreams go.
Let robots listen to the rising bell
And spring to earn their bread;
I'll yawn at the dawn and carry on
For ten more minutes in bed.

THE STRANGE CASE OF THE AMBITIOUS
CADDY

Once upon a time there was a boy named Robin
   Bideawee.

ѻ

He had chronic hiccups.

ѻ

He had hay fever, too.

ѻ

Also, he was learning to whistle through his teeth.

ѻ

Oh yes, and his shoes squeaked.

ѻ

The scoutmaster told him he had better be a caddy.

ѻ

He said, Robin, you aren't cut out for a scout, you're
   cut out for a caddy.

ѻ

At the end of Robin's first day as a caddy the caddymaster asked him how he got along.

ѻ

Robin said, I got along fine but my man lost six balls,
   am I ready yet?

ѻ

The caddymaster said No, he wasn't ready yet.

ѻ

At the end of the second day the caddymaster asked
   him again how he got along.

ѻ

Robin said, My man left me behind to look for a ball on the fourth hole and I didn't catch up to him till the eighteenth, am I ready yet?

∽

The caddymaster said No, he wasn't ready yet.

∽

Next day Robin said, I only remembered twice to take the flag on the greens and when I did take it I wiggled it, am I ready yet?

∽

The caddymaster said No, he wasn't ready yet.

∽

Next day Robin said, My man asked me whether he had a seven or an eight on the waterhole and I said an eight, am I ready yet?

∽

The caddymaster said No, he wasn't ready yet.

∽

Next day Robin said, Every time my man's ball stopped on the edge of a bunker I kicked it in, am I ready yet?

∽

The caddymaster said No, he wasn't ready yet.

∽

Next day Robin said, I never once handed my man the club he asked for, am I ready yet?

∽

The caddymaster said No, he wasn't ready yet.

∽

Next day Robin said, I bet a quarter my man would
  lose and told him so, am I ready yet?

∽

The caddymaster said, Not quite.

∽

Next day Robin said, I laughed at my man all the way
  round, am I ready yet?

∽

The caddymaster said, Have you still got hiccups, and
  have you still got hay fever, and are you still learning how to whistle through your teeth and do
  your shoes still squeak?

∽

Robin said, Yes, yes, a thousand times yes.

∽

Then you are indeed ready, said the caddymaster.

∽

Tomorrow you shall caddy for Ogden Nash.

There is one form of argument that though I am a
    voicer of I can't see the good of,

And that is, arguing that you can afford something you
    can't afford just because it doesn't cost much more
    than something you also can't afford would of.

You pass up going to the movies,

And then you suddenly pat yourselves on the back for
    passing them up and say we passed them up, there-
    fore we can afford to take dinner out and order
    a lot of hors d'ovies,

And the dinner costs five dollars, but the movies would
    have cost seventy cents,

So the dinner only really cost four-thirty which for
    the dinner you had is not so immense,

So then you say there is a new show opening tonight
    but we don't know whether it's good or terrible,
    so why take a chance,

So why not go out and dance?

So you go out and dance and the least you pay is ten
    dollars for cover charge plus elixir,

But on that basis you figure you are at least four dol-
    lars ahead on the evening because seats to an open-
    ing that anybody wants to see open are not to be
    had for a fiver or indeed a sixer,

So eventually you go to bed,

And you wake up in the morning with the glorious
    feeling that you are several dollars ahead,

So you start out the day being ahead by several dollars,

And then you read an advertisement saying that somebody has removed thirty per cent. from the price
of their ties and socks and collars,
So although the ties and socks and collars you already
have are still pretty clean,
Why you go in and order fifty dollars' worth because
by spending fifty dollars you can save fifteen,
So take the fifteen that you save on the ties and socks
and collars plus what you saved the night before
and it is obvious that you have saved about twenty,
Which for a twenty-four-hour thrift account strikes
you as plenty,
So then you really get the economical urge,
And then you really begin to splurge,
And you look on every splurge as a fairy godmother's
gift
Because you charge it all up to thrift,
Because the more you spend, the more you save, so
you naturally spend enormous amounts,
Because whether you can pay for it or not, it's the prin-
ciple of thrift that counts,
So it ends up with your starting out by saving the
seventy cents that you would have squandered
at your neighborhood cinema,
And really and truly ends up by your saving two dollars
or two thousand, depending on whether you have
spent twenty dollars or twenty thousand to save
it, which just depends on your financial maxima
and minima.

KIND OF AN ODE TO DUTY

O Duty,
Why hast thou not the visage of a sweetie or a cutie?
Why displayest thou the countenance of the kind of
    conscientious organizing spinster
That the minute you see her you are aginster?
Why glitter thy spectacles so ominously?
Why art thou clad so abominously?
Why art thou so different from Venus
And why do thou and I have so few interests mutually
    in common between us?
Why art thou fifty per cent. martyr
And fifty-one per cent. Tartar?
Why is it thy unfortunate wont
To try to attract people by calling on them either to
    leave undone the deeds they like, or to do the deeds
    they don't?
Why art thou so like an April post mortem
On something that died in the ortumn?
Above all, why dost thou continue to hound me?
Why art thou always albatrossly hanging around me?
Thou so ubiquitous,
And I so iniquitous.
I seem to be the one person in the world thou art per-
    petually preaching at who or to who;
Whatever looks like fun, there art thou standing be-
    tween me and it, calling yoo-hoo.
O Duty, Duty!
How noble a man should I be hadst thou the visage
    of a sweetie or a cutie!

Wert thou but houri instead of hag
Then would my halo indeed be in the bag!
But as it is thou art so much forbiddinger than a
    Wodehouse hero's forbiddingest aunt
That in the words of the poet, When Duty whispers
    low, Thou must, this erstwhile youth replies, i
    just can't.

There are several generally recognized grounds for divorce,

And there are moments when stealing is a starving
man's only recourse;

There are gatherings when it is perfectly proper to tell
a dubious story if there is sufficient wit in it,

And there are provocations under which it is allowable
to pull away an old lady's chair as she is about to
sit in it,

But there is one unpardonable sin and in extenuation
of it let us quote no Ballads of Reading Gaol and
in praise of it let us chant no merry madrigals,

And that is amateur theadrigals.

Now, the urge to dress up and pretend to be somebody else is a universal human weakness,

Like never going to church except on Easter and then
crowding out all the people who have been there
the other fifty-one Sundays of the year, or never
going to the races except for the Belmont or the
Preakness.

So if some alternate All-Eastern left tackle who has
been told he looks like Noel Coward wants to toss
badinage back and forth like a medicine ball with
a Junior Leaguer who has been told that with her
glasses off she looks like Gertrude Lawrence,

Why that's their business, like drinking sidecars in
bed or putting maple walnut ice cream on their
oysters, and if they kept it to themselves it could
be viewed with tolerance as well as abhorrence,

But the trouble is that they refuse to indulge their
   depraved appetites in the privacy of deserts or
   cloisters,
The kick is missing unless a lot of people are on hand
   to watch them drink sidecars in bed or put maple
   walnut ice cream on their oysters,
So they inveigle all their friends and relatives and all
   the relatives of their friends and all the friends of
   their relatives, in the name of various worthy char-
   ities,
Into paying for the privilege of sitting for three hours
   on piano stools and watching them project their
   personalities across the footlights with the gusto
   and élan of Oriental beggars exhibiting their physical peculiarities.
Tonight I am being taken to see the Troubadour Players do the Merchant of Venice.
I shall go with the same eagerness with which, if I
   weren't me, I should pay three-thirty to watch me
   play tennis.

In this fairly temperate clime
Summertime is itchy time.
O'er rocks and stumps and ruined walls
Shiny poison ivy crawls.
Every walk in woods and fields
Its aftermath of itching yields.
Hand me down my rusty hatchet;
Someone murmured, Do not scratch it.

Reason permeates my rhyme:
Summertime is itchy time.
Beneath the orange August moon
Overfed mosquitoes croon.
After sun-up, flies and midges
Raise on people bumps and ridges.
Hand me down my rusty hatchet;
Someone murmured, Do not scratch it.

Lo, the year is in its prime;
Summertime is itchy time.
People loll upon the beaches
Ripening like gaudy peaches.
Friends, the beach is not the orchard,
Nor is the peach by sunburn tortured.
Hand me down my rusty hatchet;
Someone murmured, Do not scratch it.

Now the menu is sublime;
Summertime is itchy time.

Berries, clams, and lobsters tease
Our individual allergies.
Rash in rosy splendor thrives,
Running neck-and-neck with hives.
Hand me down my rusty hatchet;
Someone murmured, Do not scratch it.

The bluebells and the cowbells chime;
Summertime is itchy time.
Despite cold soup, and ice, and thermoses
Garments cling to epidermises.
That fiery-footed centipede,
Prickly heat prowls forth to feed.
Hand me down my rusty hatchet;
Someone murmured, Do not scratch it.

Hatchet-killings ain't a crime:
Summertime is itchy time.

I'M TERRIBLY SORRY FOR YOU, BUT I CAN'T
HELP LAUGHING

Everybody has a perfect right to do what they please,

But one thing that I advise everybody not to do is to contract a laughable disease.

There is something impressive about cholera,

And anybody who undergoes an operation gets a reputation for courage even if they are a screaming cowardly hollera;

People speak of you respectfully if you catch bubonic,

And if you get typhus they think you have done something positively mastodonic;

One touch of leprosy makes the whole world your kin,

And even a slight concussion earns you an anxious inquiry and not a leering grin.

Yes, as long as people are pretty sure you have something you are going to be removed by,

Why they are very sympathetic, and books and flowers and visits and letters are what their sympathy is proved by.

But unfortunately there are other afflictions anatomical,

And people insist on thinking that a lot of them are comical,

And if you are afflicted with this kind of affliction people are amused and disdainful,

Because they are not bright enough to realize that an affliction can be ludicrous and still be ominous and painful.

Suppose for instance you have a dreadful attack of
    jaundice, what do they do?
They come around and smile and say Well well, how
    are you today, Dr. Fu-Manchu?
The early martyrs thought they knew what it was to be
    taken over the jumps,
But no martyr really ought to get his diploma until he
    has undergone his friends' witticisms during his
    mumps.
When you have laryngitis they rejoice,
Because apparently the funniest thing in the world
    is when you can't curse and swear at them for
    laughing at your lost voice, because you have lost
    your voice.
Toothache is another diversion that hearty amuse-
    ment yields,
And if you have a severe enough case of sunburn they
    find you funnier than W. C. Fields.
And as for boils,
Well, my pen recoils,
Because people's invariable humorous remarks about
    other people's boils are invariably unprintable,
And most of them are not even hintable.
So I advise you, at the risk of being pedantic,
If you must be sick, by all means choose a sickness
    that is preferably fatal and certainly romantic,
Because it is much better to have that kind of sickness
    and be sick unto death or anyway half to death,
Than to have the other kind and be laughed to death.

WHERE THERE'S A WILL, THERE'S VELLEITY

Seated one day at the dictionary I was pretty weary
    and also pretty ill at ease,

Because a word I had always liked turned out not to
    be a word at all, and suddenly I found myself
    among the v's,

And suddenly among the v's I came across a new word
    which was a word called velleity,

So the new word I found was better than the old word
    I lost, for which I thank my tutelary deity,

Because velleity is a word which gives me great satis-
    faction,

Because do you know what it means, it means low degree
    of volition not prompting to action,

And I always knew I had something holding me back
    but I didn't know what,

And it's quite a relief to know it isn't a conspiracy,
    it's only velleity that I've got,

Because to be wonderful at everything has always been
    my ambition,

Yes indeed, I am simply teeming with volition,

So why I never was wonderful at anything was some-
    thing I couldn't see

While all the time, of course, my volition was merely
    volition of a low degree,

Which is the kind of volition that you are better off
    without it,

Because it puts an idea in your head but doesn't prompt
    you to do anything about it.

So you think it would be nice to be a great pianist but
     why bother with practising for hours at the key-
     board,
Or you would like to be the romantic captain of a
     romantic ship but can't find time to study naviga-
     tion or charts of the ocean or the seaboard;
You want a lot of money but you are not prepared to
     work for it,
Or a book to read in bed but you do not care to go
     into the nocturnal cold and murk for it;
And now if you have any such symptoms you can
     identify your malady with accurate spontaneity:
It's velleity,
So don't forget to remember that you're velleitous, and
     if anybody says you're just lazy,
Why, they're crazy.

Once upon a time there was a man named Mr. Sponsoon who was highly ineffectual.

෴

He always looked as if he were growing a moustache.

෴

His singing voice was pretty fair except for the high notes.

෴

Oh yes, and the low notes, too.

෴

One day he was driving along the street when he saw a beautiful girl.

෴

My, what a beautiful girl, said Mr. Sponsoon. I wish I knew her name.

෴

If I asked her her name, said Mr. Sponsoon, she might think me a brazen cad.

෴

But if I don't know her name, she will go out of my life forever.

෴

Mr. Sponsoon thought and thought.

෴

Suppose I run over her gently, he thought at last.

෴

With one wheel, say.

෴

Certainly with no more than two.

∽

Then I can read her name in the morning paper and
all will be hotsy-totsy.

∽

Mr. Sponsoon pointed his car at the beautiful girl.

∽

The beautiful girl leaped like a thoroughbred gazelle.

∽

Mr. Sponsoon chased her for seven blocks and never
laid a wheel on her.

∽

In the middle of the eighth block she stopped to moisten
her finger on account of a run in her stocking.

∽

Mr. Sponsoon read in the morning paper that her
name was Shella Schminck and she was in Percy's
Hospital.

∽

So he went to the Mercy Hospital and asked for Stella
Smith.

∽

To the girl o' his dreams he explained his little strat-
agem.

∽

Girl o' my dreams, I had to know your name, said
Mr. Sponsoon, avoiding high notes and low notes.

∽

Say you forgive me, girl o' my dreams,

∽

Say all is hotsy-totsy.

ᐧᐧᐧ

The girl o' Mr. Sponsoon's dreams said all was far from hotsy-totsy.

ᐧᐧᐧ

All was coldsy-toldsy, said the girl o' Mr. Sponsoon's dreams.

ᐧᐧᐧ

Mr. Sponsoon joined the Foreign Legion, but was soon expelled because he admitted he liked it.

ᐧᐧᐧ

When last heard of, he was borrowing a burnt cork from Amos and Andy.

ᐧᐧᐧ

He said he had decided to steal into Rome as an Ethiopian spy.

FELLOW CREATURES

I

THE CALF

Pray, butcher, spare yon tender calf!
Accept my plea on his behalf;
He's but a babe, too young by far
To perish in the abattoir.
Oh, cruel butcher, let him feed
And gambol on the verdant mead;
Let clover tops and grassy banks
Fill out those childish ribs and flanks.
Then may we, at some future meal,
Pitch into beef, instead of veal.

II

THE PURIST

I give you now Professor Twist,
A conscientious scientist.
Trustees exclaimed, "He never bungles!"
And sent him off to distant jungles.
Camped on a tropic riverside.
One day he missed his loving bride.
She had, the guide informed him later,
Been eaten by an alligator.
Professor Twist could not but smile.
"You mean," he said, "a crocodile."

THE ANT

The ant has made himself illustrious
Through constant industry industrious.
So what?
Would you be calm and placid
If you were full of formic acid?

THE HIPPOPOTAMUS

Behold the hippopotamus!
We laugh at how he looks to us.
And yet in moments dank and grim
I wonder how we look to him.
Peace, peace, thou hippopotamus!
We really look all right to us,
As you no doubt delight the eye
Of other hippopotami.

THE CENTIPEDE

I objurgate the centipede,
A bug we do not really need.
At sleepy-time he beats a path
Straight to the bedroom or the bath.
You always wallop where he's not,
Or, if he is, he makes a spot.

Christmas time used to be the time when everybody
    loved everybody,
And even in the subway when everybody had their
    arms full of packages nobody shoved everybody.
People went around looking benevolent,
And good will was pleasingly prevalent,
And the cockles of people's hearts were all warm and
    cockley
And crisp new bills were scattered on elevator boys
    like broccoli,
And people had grandmothers and were fond of their
    family,
And the weather acted more New Englandly and less
    Miamily,
And on Christmas Eve people would assemble their
    friends and merrily sing carols with them and
    merrily congeal with them,
And they sent Christmas cards and presents to people
    because they liked them and not because they
    hoped to put over a deal with them.
Yes, the good old Yuletide was indeed sublime,
But that was once upon a time,
Because now everybody has somebody they are trying
    to blow to pieces or dismember,
And people can't concentrate properly on blowing other
    people to pieces properly if their minds are poisoned
    by thoughts suitable to the twenty-fifth of De-
    cember.
Hence my thesis,

Which is that I think it is much nicer to have a nice
    Christmas than to blow somebody to pesis,
So please excuse me for a moment while I momentarily
    take my mind off Tokio and Peiping and the Rebels
    and the Loyalists;
Forgive me if I temporarily ignore the disagreement
    between Mr. Lewis and the Economic Royalists;
This is not the season for tales of Der Fuehrer and
    his sportsmanship;
Call again on the twenty-sixth if you want to discuss
    the Chief Executive and his Supreme Courtsman-
    ship;
Christmas comes but once every Anno Domini,
And I want an old-fashioned one and I invite every-
    body who is on my side to enjoy it the way it
    ought to be enjoyed even though everybody on
    the other side will undoubtedly cover us with ig-
    nominy.

JANGLE BELLS

Man is said to want but little here below,
And I have an idea that what he wants littlest of is
snow.
Snow is all right while it is snowing;
It is like inebriation because it is very pleasing when
it is coming, but very unpleasing when it is going,
But any further resemblance between the two has
escaped this Old Master,
Because certainly everybody would rather be sozzled
than snowbound, except maybe Mrs. Ella Boole
and Lady Astor.
Snow is what you are up to your neck in when people
send you post cards from Florida saying they wish
you were there, and I wish they might sit on a
burr,
Because they don't wish anything of the kind, no, they
are secretly glad you are not there, otherwise they
couldn't send the post card saying they wish you
were.

Some people understand all about machinery,
And to them it is just like beautiful poetry or beautiful
    scenery,
Because they know how to control and handle it,
Because they understandle it,
Yes, when they are confronted with a complicated piece
    of machinery,
Why, they are as cool and collected as a dean sitting in
    his deanery,
And I certainly wish I were among them because if
    there is one thing that makes me terrified and pan-
    ical,
It is anything mechanical and nowadays everything is
    mechanical.
O thrice unhappy home
Whose master doesn't know the difference between a
    watt and an ohm!
O radio glum and silent as a glum and silent burial
When no one knows what to do about the grounding
    or the aerial!
O four-door sedan cantankerous and stubborn and
    Mad Hattery,
With none to give a thought to occasionally changing
    the oil or once in a while checking on the bat-
    tery!
O telephone and vacuum cleaners and cameras and
    electric toasters and streamlined locomotives and
    artificial refrigeration,

O thermostats and elevators and cigarette-lighters and
    air-conditioning units and all ye other gadgets that
    make ours a mighty nation,
I think you are every one a miracle,
And you do wonderful things and it's probably only
    because I don't see how you do what you do that
    when I think of you I become hystirical,
And of course that is silly of me because what does
    it matter how you function so long as all I have
    to do to get you to function is push a button or
    throw a switch,
Always assuming that I can remember which is which,
So keep on functioning, please,
Because if you don't I shall starve or freeze.

THE LOST CAUSE

There is nothing like a rousing slogan
For releasing necks from a tyrant's brogan;
Victory blooms from latent rout
At the lilt of a leader's well-phrased shout;
Dying men will forget to die
And obey a catchy battlecry.
Indeed, you may sway the swirling crowd
With any order sufficiently loud;
You may break a kingdom and gain a crown,
But you cannot make a crowd sit down.

O, down in front! Down in front!
The people behind implore.
There are giants to right and giants to left,
And Siamese giants before.
A halfback wriggles through the line,
A tackle blocks a punt,
The stadium rocks to thrills and shocks
And the cry of Down in Front!
Sit down, sit down, the game grows frantic!
But the giants only grow more gigantic.

You people in front can see already;
You're sitting pretty; why not sit steady?
It's the people in front who stand up first,
And then expand till you hope they burst.
The people in front are all colossuses
With the bulk and also the hide of rhinocuses.

The little people sit behind;
They meekly and weakly go it blind,
Till at last they rise in brash defiance,
And what do you know? They too are giants!

O, down in front! Down in front!
The age-old slogan rings,
But the human elephants rise to their feet
As the desperate slugger swings.
The pitcher waves the fielders back,
The runners shuffle and shunt,
And fans who seethe and fail to breathe
Must yet cry Down in front!
Sit down, sit down, and a happy landing!
And all the elephants keep on standing.

AWAY FROM IT ALL

I wish I were a Thibetan monk
Living in a monastery.
I would unpack my trunk
And store it in a tronastery;
I would collect all my junk
And send it to a jonastery;
I would try to reform a drunk,
And pay his expenses at a dronastery.
And if my income shrunk
I would send it to a shronastery.

Upon a peak in Darien
The Sage surveys his fellow men,
Exerting to its full capacity
His preternatural sagacity.
Sore eyes and empty stomach mutiny;
The Sage confines himself to scrutiny,
Occasionally sniffing through a tube
The vapor of a bouillon cube.
Thus, all his grosser instincts chastening,
He thinks to bring the vision hastening.
The truth about his fellow men,
He hopes, will bloom within his ken.
At last appears a tiny truth,
A sliver like a baby's tooth.
Now fast it grows, it swells, it waxes,
It multiplies itself like taxes.
The ultimate truth, for what it's worth,
Crowds minor truthlets off the earth.
The Sage cries Bother! through his beard;
Says he, Exactly what I feared.
I needn't have come to Darien
To scrutinize my fellow men;
It seems I've scaled this natural steeple
To learn what I've always known about people.
To confirm through sacrifice intense
The fact that people have no sense.
People are born in pain and woe,
In woe and pain through life they go,
Harpies attend their to-and-froing,

And yet the blockheads keep on going.
Dictators tread upon their necks,
And presidents their purses vex,
Republics rob them, monarchies milk them,
Revolutions unfailingly bilk them;
Tyrants imprison them and slaughter them;
Promoters take their stocks and water them;
Statements and bills pile high around them;
Sheriffs and credit departments hound them;
By ten-ton trucks they are forced from the roads;
Every October they change their abodes;
Frequent expensive diseases smite them;
Sunbeams burn them, mosquitoes bite them;
Employers jeer at their shiny diplomas;
Advertisers insult their aromas;
People are born in pain and woe,
In woe and pain through life they go;
They have no cause at all for thanksgiving.
And yet the idiots keep on living.
Upon a peak in Darien
The Sage renounced his fellow men.
His fellow men he did renounce,
And leapt, and lit, and didn't bounce.

Many people have asked me what was the most beauti-
    ful sight I saw during the recent summer,

And I think the most beautiful sight was the day the
    water wouldn't stop running and in came the
    plumber,

Because your cottage may be very cunning,

But you don't appreciate it when the water won't stop
    running,

And you would almost rather submit to burgling

Than to consistent gurgling.

And then the other most beautiful sight I saw during
    the summer

Was the day the water wouldn't run at all and in came
    the plumber,

Because one thing even less enticing than a mess of
    pottage

Is a waterless cottage,

So apparently all my beautiful memories of the summer

Are beautiful memories of the plumber,

And I am sorry they aren't more romantic,

I am sorry they are not memories of the moonlight
    rippling on the Atlantic,

Oh my yes, what wouldn't I give for some beautiful
    memories of the fields and the sky and the sea,

But they are not for the likes of me,

Nay, if you want to have beautiful memories of the
    summer,

Why the thing to do is to be a plumber,

Because then you can have some really beautiful beauties to remember,

Because naturally plumbers wouldn't think plumbers were the most beautiful thing they saw between June and September,

And that's the great advantage plumbers have over me and you,

They don't have to think about plumbers, so they can concentrate on the view.

Dear friends, I am agitated because the world is so
full of a number of things that puzzle me,

And you are sadly mistaken if you think that any
craven fear of displaying my ignorance is going
to muzzle me.

Now, you take the way of a ship on the sea, or
the way of a man with a maid, or the way of an
eagle,

And I can follow them like a beagle,

And I can also understand the way of Achilles with
the maidens and the way of Br'er Rabbit and Br'er
Fox and Br'er Possum,

But I will be the Burial of Sir John Moore at Corunna
if I understand the way of people who go around
saying they Would God they were a tender appleblossom.

As a rule I deprecate severity,

But I must say that when I hear anybody saying Would
to God they were a tender appleblossom I question their sincerity.

In the first place if they were an appleblossom at all,
why to them it would be one

Whether they were tender or tough or rare or well
done.

And one thing more:

What do they want to be any kind of appleblossom
for?

Presumably they want to be an appleblossom because
  they are in love, but appleblossoms never get to
  stand up beside their beloved in church or chapel,
No, the most romantic thing that happens to appleblossoms is that once in a while they grow up to
  be an apple,
So I'd like to know what the country is coming to and
  I think we ought to discuss it,
Because I am afraid all the younger generation that
  used to want to grow up to be president or a movie
  star or a fireman will now set their hearts on growing up to be a pippin or a russet.
Loose talk is loose talk, whether it emanates from Washington or Palo Alto,
And somehow it seems even looser when it emanates
  from either a male or female contralto,
And loose talkers are something that we have more
  than ample of,
And I think it high time that some of them were made
  an example of,
So I certainly hope and pray
That sometime soon somebody will be in love with a
  handsome young neurologist and will say Would
  God they were a tender appleblossom and they will
  get their wish and turn into a tender appleblossom
  and then ripen into an apple and then keep the
  doctor away.

THE POLITICIAN

Behold the politician.
Self-preservation is his ambition.
He thrives in the D. of C.,
Where he was sent by you and me.

Whether elected or appointed
He considers himself the Lord's anointed,
And indeed the ointment lingers on him
So thick you can't get your fingers on him.

He has developed a sixth sense
About living at the public expense,
Because in private competition
He would encounter malnutrition.

He has many profitable hobbies
Not the least of which is lobbies.
He would not sell his grandmother for a quarter
If he suspected the presence of a reporter.

He gains votes ever and anew
By taking money from everybody and giving it to a
    few,
While explaining that every penny
Was extracted from the few to be given to the many.

Some politicians are Republican, some Democratic,
And their feud is dramatic,
But except for the name
They are identically the same.

When a politician talks the foolishest,
And obstructs everything the mulishest,
And bellows the loudest,
Why his constituents are the proudest.

Wherever decent intelligent people get together
They talk about politicians as about bad weather,
But they are always too decent to go into politics them-
    selves and too intelligent even to go to the polls.
So I hope the kind of politicians they get will have
    no mercy on their pocketbooks or souls.

ABSENCE MAKES THE HEART GROW
HEART TROUBLE

I know a girl who is in Paris, France,
And I fear that every evening she goes out to dance,
And she ought to be pining for the undersigned,
But I fear that nothing is further from her mind,
And what is very suspicious, her letters say that she
*   is being very quiet,*
But my nerves deny it,
And I am unhappily sure that she is drinking champagne
*   with aristocrats,*
And exchanging cynicisms with sophistocrats.
She goes walking in the Bois
With elegant young men who are not moi.
She is receiving compliments from ambassadors,
And riding in fiacres with foreign agents who cry that
*   for her they would betray the secrets of their lords*
*   and massadors.*
Artists to have her pose for them are clamoring,
Tenors and symphony conductors tempt her with their
*   entire repertoire from Pagliacci to Götterdämmer*
*   ung;*
Argentines and Brazilians
Seek to dazzle her with their dazzling millions;
Men of the world with etchings and monocles
Plead with her to become part of their personal chron-
*   icles;*
Aides and equerries try to explain without too much
*   bluntness and yet without too much shyness*

The advantages a girl or a tailor enjoys when he or she
   is entitled to the subtitle of By Appointment to
   His Royal Highness.
Trips abroad are very nice for Davis Cup teams and
   Olympic teams, and that's about all you can say
   for them,
Because I think that when you are fond of somebody
   you would rather be with them than away from
   them,
So I wish that time would suddenly advance,
Because I want to be standing on the dock trying to
   find somebody on deck who will undoubtedly be
   wearing a terribly smart and perfectly terrible hat
   which she bought in Paris, France.

OUT IS OUT

Come in, dear guests, we've got a treat for you,
We've prepared a different place to eat for you!
Guess where we're going to have our dinner!
Everyone guess! Who'll be the winner?
The dining room? Heavens! It's hereby stated
That dining rooms are dreadfully dated.
What in the world could be more plebeian
Than to eat in a place in which you can see in?
The living room? No, you're off the path;
No, not the bedroom; no, not the bath;
And not the cellar; and not the attic;
The kitchen? No, that's too democratic.
Do you all give up? Well, listen and hark:
We're going to dine outdoors, in the dark!
We're going to dine outdoors, on the terrace,
As dark as an Anti-Kink heir or heiress.
No lights, because there aren't any plugs,
And anyhow, lights attract the bugs,
And anyhow, in the dark we've found
There are bugs enough to go around.
Oh, it's drizzling a little; I think perhaps
The girls had better keep on their wraps;
Just strike a match and enjoy the way
The raindrops splash in the consommé.
You probably won't get botts or pellagra
From whatever lit on your pâté de foie gras.
Now, you're not expected to eat with skill,
And everybody's supposed to spill;
If your half-broiled chicken leaps about,

That's half the excitement of eating out;
If you dust it with sugar instead of salt,
It's everyone's fun and nobody's fault;
And if anything flies in your mouth, perchance,
Why, that is mystery, that's romance!
Such a frolic and such a lark
It is to eat outdoors in the dark!
The dandiest fun since I don't know when;
Would you eat in a stuffy old room again?
Oh yes you would, you lukewarm liars,
And I'll see you tomorrow at the cleaner's and dyer's.

I am tired of gadgets with cocktails,
I am awfully tired of gadgets with cocktails,
My heart leaps down when I behold gadgets with cock-
    tails
With me they have outlived their popularity.
Gadgets with cocktails are stultified
Gadgets with cocktails are stertorous
Gadgets with cocktails are stark and stagnant
And for them I have no patience or charity.

I don't want any toast covered with vulcanized caviar
Or any soggy popcorn covered with cheesy butter or
    buttery cheese,
I don't want any potato chips or Tiny Tootsie pretzels
    or pretzel sticks,
And I don't want any crackers coated with meat paste
    or bargain pâté de foie gras particularly please.

Do not hand me that plate filled with olives unripe
    and overripe,
Anchovies whether curled or uncurled I have concluded
    not to abide,
Kindly mail all those salted peanuts and almonds to
    the Collector of Internal Revenue,
As well as all the little heart-shaped sandwiches filled
    with squashy stuff that when you pick them up they
    squirt out at the side.

Maybe somewhere there is somebody who would like
    the stuffed eggs and diminutive frankfurters,

Or who could look the stuffed celery in the eye and
　　voluntarily chew it,
Maybe there is a Chinaman in China who would care
　　for that slab of fumigated salmon,
And that thing whatever it is all rolled up with a tooth-
　　pick sticking through it.

Hostesses never tire of gadgets with cocktails,
Hostesses sit around thinking up new gadgets with cock-
　　tails,
They prowl through the papers hunting tricky gadg-
　　ets for cocktails,
And if they don't serve more than other hostesses they
　　are swamped with humiliation and grief;
Gadgets with cocktails to you, my dear Mrs. Marsh-
　　mallow,
Gadgets with cocktails to you, Mrs. Rodney St. Rodney,
Gadgets with cocktails to you and all other hostesses,
And I'll take some bread and butter and a slice of rare
　　roast beef.

There is one form of life to which I unconditionally
    surrender,
Which is the feminine gender.
Like lightning and thunder, women are awe-inspiring
    phenomena,
And they have a custom which many men might well
    adopt, which is to gird themselves in devices that
    reduce or at least repress their abdomena,
And they have a traditional rite which is handed down
    from mother to daughter,
Which is that they always have to wash their face with
    cold cream instead of water.
Also, I think there must be some great difference in the
    way men and women are built,
Because women walk around all day wearing shoes that
    a man would break his neck the first step he took
    in them because where a man's shoe has a heel
    a woman's shoe has a stilt,
So I often wonder who started this rumor about woman
    being the clinging vine and man the mighty oak
    or elm,
And I have an idea that the phrase "weaker sex" was
    coined by some woman to disarm some man she
    was preparing to overwhelm,
Because certainly a man shod like a woman would just
    have to sit down all day, and yet my land!
Women not only don't have to sit, but prefer to stand,
Because their pleasure in standing up is exquisite,

As everybody knows who has ever watched a woman pay
    a call or a visit,
Because at first they will sit in a chair,
And their heart may be in the highlands, but it certainly
    isn't there,
And their conversation is unspontaneous,
And their topics are trifling and miscellaneous,
But finally, after an uncomfortable while,
Their faces brighten with the well-I-must-be-running-
    along-now smile,
And they get to their feet and the front door,
And the Old Mother of Waters surges over the levee
    with a roar,
Because the proportions of feminine social chitchat are
    constant, always;
One part of sitting down in the sitting room to four
    parts standing up saying good-by in foyers and
    hallways,
Which is why I think that when it comes to physical
    prowess,
Why woman is a wow, or should I say a wowess.

Oh, sometimes I sit around and think, what would you
    do if you were up a dark alley and there was Caesar
    Borgia,
And he was coming torgia,
And brandished a poisoned poniard,
And looked at you like an angry fox looking at the
    plumpest rooster in a boniard?
Why that certainly would be an adventure,
It would be much more exciting than writing a poem
    or selling a debenture,
But would you be fascinated,
Or just afraid of being assassinated?
Or suppose you went out dancing some place where you
    generally dance a lot,
And you jostled somebody accidentally and it turned
    out to be Sir Lancelot,
And he drew his sword,
Would you say Have at you! or would you say Oh
    Lord!?
Or what if you were held up by a bandit,
And he told you to hand over your money, would you
    try to disarm him and turn him over to the police,
    or would you over just meekly hand it?
What would you do if you were in a luxurious cosmo-
    politan hotel surrounded by Europeans and French-
    men,
And a beautiful woman came up to you and asked you
    to rescue her from some mysterious master mind
    and his sinister henchmen?

Would you chivalrously make her rescue your personal
    objective,
Or would you refer her to the house detective?
Yes, and what if you were on trial for murdering some-
    body whom for the sake of argument we might
    call Kelly or O'Connor,
And you were innocent but were bound to be convicted
    unless you told the truth and the truth would tar-
    nish a lady's honor,
Would you elect to die like a gentleman or live like a
    poltroon,
Or put the whole thing in the hands of an arbitration
    committee headed by Heywood Broun?
Yes, often as through life I wander
This is the kind of question I ponder,
And what puzzles me most is why I even bother to pon-
    der when I already know the answer,
Because anybody who won't cross the street till the
    lights are green would never get far as a Musketeer
    or a Bengal Lancer.

Once there was a man, and he was named Mr. Barca-
　　low, to be exact,
And he prided himself on his tact,
And he said, One thing about an apple, it may have a
　　worm in it, and one thing about a chimney, it may
　　have soot in it,
But one thing about my mouth, I never put my foot
　　in it.
Now never was Mr. Barcalow's tact so exquisite
As when he went for a visit,
Because whenever he entered a community
He inquired of his host and hostess what topics he
　　could discuss with impunity,
So no matter beside whom he was deposited,
Why, he could talk to them without disturbing any
　　skeletons that should have been kept closeted,
But one dire day he went to visit some friends,
And he started asking tactful questions about untactful
　　conversational trends,
And his host said that here was one place that Mr. Bar-
　　calow wouldn't need his tact,
Because taboos and skeletons were what everybody there
　　lacked,
And his hostess said, That's right, but you'd better not
　　mention bathrooms to Emily, who you will sit by
　　at lunch,
Because her grandmother was scalded to death in a
　　shower shortly after complaining that there was
　　no kick in the punch,

And his host said, Oh yes, and steer away from education when you talk to the Senator,

Because somebody said his seventeen-year-old nephew would have to burn down the schoolhouse to get out of the third grade and his nephew overheard them and did burn down the schoolhouse, including the music teacher and the janitor,

And his hostess said, Oh yes, and if you talk about love and marriage to Mrs. Musker don't be surprised if her eye sort of wanders,

Because her daughter is the one who had the divorce suit with thirty-seven co-responders,

And his host said, Oh yes, and you'd better know that the war is Florence's mania,

Because her cousin-in-law was the man who sank the Lusitania,

And Mr. Barcalow said, Well, can I talk about sports,

And his hostess said, Well maybe you'd better not because Louise's sister, the queer one, was asked to resign from the club because she went out to play moonlight tennis in shorts, and Mr. Barcalow said That's not so terrible is it, everybody wears shorts, and his hostess said, Yes, but she forgot the shorts,

So Mr. Barcalow said Well then, what about the weather,

And his host said Well, that's what we used to discuss when we got together,

But it has recently become a pleasure we must defer,

Because Jane's Aunt Julia is here from California and she seems to think every remark about the weather is a personal affront to her.

So Mr. Barcalow said, The hell with you all, and went
    upstairs and packed,
And that was the last that was ever heard of Mr. Barca-
    low and his tact.

You have your hat and coat on and she says she will
    be right down,

And you hope so because it is getting late and you are
    dining on the other side of town,

And you are pretty sure she can't take long,

Because when you left her she already looked as neat
    and snappy as a Cole Porter song,

So you stand around thinking of various things and
    wondering why good rye costs more than Scotch,

And after a while you begin to look at your watch,

And so goes ten minutes, and then fifteen minutes, and
    then half an hour,

And you listen for the sound of water running because
    you suspect she may have gone back for a bath or
    a shower,

Or maybe she is taking a nap,

Or possibly getting up a subscription for the benefit of
    the children of the mouse that she said mean things
    about last night but she is now sorry got caught in
    a trap,

Or maybe she decided her hair was a mess and is now
    shampooing it,

But whatever she is up to, she is a long time doing it,

And finally she comes down and says she is sorry she
    couldn't find the right lipstick, that's why she was
    so slow,

And you look at her and she looks marvelous but not
    a bit more marvelous than she did when you left
    her forty-five minutes ago,

And you tell her she looks ravishing and she says No,
    she is a sight,
And you reflect that you are now an hour late, but at
    any rate she is now groomed for the rest of the
    night,
So you get to your destination and there's the ladies'
    dressing room and before you know it she's in it,
But she says she'll be back in a minute,
And so she is, but not to tarry,
No, only to ask you for her bag, which she has forgot-
    ten she had asked you to carry,
So you linger in the lobby
And wish you had a nice portable hobby,
And you try to pass the time seeing how much you can
    remember of the poetry you learned in school, both
    good verse and bad verse,
And eventually she re-appears just about as you have de-
    cided she was in the middle of Anthony Adverse,
And she doesn't apologize, but glances at you as if you
    were Bluebeard or Scrooge,
And says why didn't you tell her she had on too much
    rouge?
And you look to see what new tint she has acquired,
And she looks just the same as she did before she re-
    tired,
So you dine, and reach the theater in time for the third
    act, and then go somewhere to dance and sup,
And she says she looks like a scarecrow, she has to go
    straighten up,
So then you don't see her for quite a long time,

But at last you see her for a moment when she comes
out to ask if you will lend her a dime,

The moral of all which is that you will have just as
much of her company and still save considerable
on cover charges and beverages and grub

If instead of taking her out on the town, you settle her in
a nice comfortable dressing room and then go off
and spend the evening at the Club.

CONFESSIONS OF A BORN SPECTATOR

One infant grows up and becomes a jockey,
Another plays basketball or hockey,
This one the prize ring hastes to enter,
That one becomes a tackle or center.
I'm just as glad as glad can be
That I'm not them, that they're not me.

With all my heart do I admire
Athletes who sweat for fun or hire,
Who take the field in gaudy pomp
And maim each other as they romp;
My limp and bashful spirit feeds
On other people's heroic deeds.

Now A runs ninety yards to score;
B knocks the champion to the floor;
C, risking vertebrae and spine,
Lashes his steed across the line.
You'd think my ego it would please
To swap positions with one of these.

Well, ego might be pleased enough,
But zealous athletes play so rough;
They do not ever, in their dealings,
Consider one another's feelings.
I'm glad that when my struggle begins
Twixt prudence and ego, prudence wins.

When swollen eye meets gnarled fist,
When snaps the knee, and cracks the wrist,
When calm officialdom demands,
Is there a doctor in the stands?
My soul in true thanksgiving speaks
For this most modest of physiques.

Athletes, I'll drink to you or eat with you,
Or anything except compete with you;
Buy tickets worth their weight in radium
To watch you gambol in a stadium,
And reassure myself anew
That you're not me and I'm not you.

Steamer, steamer, outward bound,
Couldn't you, wouldn't you turn around?
Mightn't you double on your track?
Mightn't you possibly bring her back?
No, says the steamer, No, no, no!
We go, says the steamer, go, go, go!
Who, says the steamer, Who are you?
Boo! says the steamer.
Boo!

Steamer, steamer, are you sure
You can carry her secure?
Emerge from ice and storm and fog
With an uneventful log?
Chance, says the steamer, I am chance!
Chance, says the steamer, That's romance!
Who, says the steamer, Who are you?
Boo! says the steamer.
Boo!

Steamer, steamer, hard and splendid,
Goddess unwittingly offended,
Are the males who prowl your decks
Attractive to the other sex?
Wait, says the steamer, Sit and wait.
Fate, says the steamer, I am Fate.
Who, says the steamer, Who are you?
Boo! says the steamer.
Boo!

Steamer, cogitate a while,
Before you smile your final smile.
Seven days are yours to mock;
Steamer, wait until you dock.
Wait till she is safe ashore,
Steamer I do not adore!
Boo, says the steamer, and double boo!
Who, says the steamer,
Are you?

Steamer, steamer, I am he
Whose raison d'être you bore to sea,
And I wish you junkets and week-end cruises
With passenger lists of Nazis and Jewses,
Of Hyde Park Roosevelts, beamish and gay,
And Roosevelts from Oyster Bay.
Steamer, lightly you weighed your anchor.
Try so lightly to weigh my rancor.
You who carried her off so boldly
Shall pay for it hotly, pay for it coldly,
With blistering hurricanes, frosty gales,
With amateur octopods, crooning whales —
Steamer, as soon as she is off you,
Then I shall really cut loose and scoff you!
Steamer, when she has tipped the purser,
I'll curse you meaner, I'll curse you worser,
Pooh! says the steamer, Pooh for you!
Toodle-de-oodle-de-oo!

THE INTRODUCTION

This is Mr. Woolley, Mrs. Nixon;
This is Mrs. Nixon, Mr. Woolley;
Mr. Woolley, Mrs. Nixon is a vixen;
Mrs. Nixon, Mr. Woolley is a bully.
Shake hands with Mr. Woolley, Mrs. Nixon;
Shake hands with Mrs. Nixon, Mr. Woolley;
And let the welkin shout that it's I who brought **about**
The meeting of the vixen and the bully.

Mrs. Nixon is one of those ladies
With a disposition acquired in Hades.
What! you exclaim. That placid blonde?
She's as shallow and calm as a lily pond!
I've seen her at parties, at dances, at teas,
Her crossest command is, If you please.
Well, give her a racquet and bulging shorts
And put her out on the tennis courts;
Then, if you care to behold your vixen,
Give her for partner Mr. Nixon.
Hark to her shrill and furious cries
As she damns his hands and feet and eyes.
It's mine! she shrieks. She swings and misses.
Why didn't you get it, you swine? she hisses.
She explains to the world her vagrant serves;
Her clumsy partner upsets her nerves.
He scores a placement. Says she, A miracle!
He doesn't. She rocks with mirth hystirical.
Over the backstop, into the net
She angrily lollops game and set,

And sweetly barks, when the match is through,
We're beaten again, dear, thanks to you.

Mr. Woolley, oh Mr. Woolley!
Hell will welcome him warmly, fully.
What! you exclaim. That genial fellow?
He's a chivalrous gentleman, mild and mellow.
Around the club, from lip to lip,
Run tales of his generous sportsmanship.
Well, if your stomach is strong and able,
Set him down at a contract table;
Then, if you care to behold your bully,
Give him for partner Mrs. Woolley.
She should have bid, or she shouldn't have bid,
She shouldn't have done whatever she did.
Does she hold a hand? He bids it away;
He'd rather go down than let her play.
A celluloid duck, he loudly avers,
Might boast of better brains than hers.
And oft, with polished wit sardonic,
He hails her as Poison, or Bubonic,
Or else with humor gay and easy,
Hopes she's enjoying her parcheesi.
He roars, with the last lost rubber concluded;
We've lost ten dollars, and that's what you did.

Oh, this is Mrs. Woolley, Mr. Nixon,
And this is Mr. Nixon, Mrs. Woolley;
Mrs. Woolley, Mrs. Nixon is a vixen;
Mrs. Nixon, Mr. Woolley is a bully.

Shake hands with Mrs. Woolley, Mr. Nixon;
Shake hands with Mr. Nixon, Mrs. Woolley;
To both of you more power, and may your meeting
    flower
In the slaughter of a vixen and a bully.

RIDING ON A RAILROAD TRAIN

Some people like to hitch and hike;
They are fond of highway travel;
Their nostrils toil through gas and oil,
They choke on dust and gravel.
Unless they stop for the traffic cop
Their road is a fine-or-jail road,
But wise old I go rocketing by;
I'm riding on the railroad.

I love to loll like a limp rag doll
In a peripatetic salon;
To think and think of a long cool drink
And cry to the porter, allons!
Now the clickety clack of wheel on track
Grows clickety clackety clicker:
The line is clear for the engineer
And it mounts to his head like liquor.

Oh give me steel from roof to wheel,
But a soft settee to sit on,
And a cavalcade of commerce and trade
And a drummer to turn the wit on.
Stuyvesant chats with Kelly and Katz,
The professor warms to the broker,
And life is good in the brotherhood

Of an air-conditioned smoker.
With a farewell scream of escaping steam
The boiler bows to the Diesel;
The Iron Horse has run its course

And we ride a chromium weasel;
We draw our power from the harnessed shower,
The lightning without the thunder,
But a train is a train and will so remain
While the rails glide glistening under.

Oh, some like trips in luxury ships,
And some in gasoline wagons,
And others swear by the upper air
And the wings of flying dragons.
Let each make haste to indulge his taste,
Be it beer, champagne or cider;
My private joy, both man and boy,
Is being a railroad rider.

*Every schoolboy is taught by his teacher, if not by his
   mother,*

*That things which are equal to the same thing are
   equal to each other,*

*But that is a lesson of which every schoolboy should be
   an eschewer,*

Because almost nothing could be untruer,

*Because even if it is partly true there is one point where
   its veracity ends,*

And that is the point of your friends.

Now we can assume without any fuss

That all our friends are equal to us,

And we do not have to haw and hem

In stating that we are equal to all of them,

So therefore according to our teacher or our mother,

*All our friends are equal to the same thing, which is us,
   so they ought to be equal to each other,*

But it is my complaint

That they ain't.

*You have two favorite friends and they have never met
   each other and you are dying to have them meet
   each other,*

*And you bring them together and stand back anxiously
   while they greet each other,*

*And you think it is going to be a big treat, but no treat
   could be littler,*

*Because the meeting is about as genial as a meeting of
   Rabbi Wise and Hitler,*

And disapproval is rampant,

And your enthusiasm for introducing your friends to
    each other is dampent,
But these meetings aren't over when they are through,
No, because all your friends go around blaming all
    your other friends on you,
And the way it ends
Is that not only do your friends fail to fraternize, but
    they stop being friends with you, because they can't
    stand your friends,
So if you have a couple of friends who are very close
    to your heart,
For heaven's sake keep them apart,
Because otherwise I take my oath
You're going to lose 'em both.

One thing I like less than most things is sitting in a den-
    tist chair with my mouth wide open,
And that I will never have to do it again is a hope that
    I am against hope hopen.
Because some tortures are physical and some are mental,
But the one that is both is dental.
It is hard to be self-possessed
With your jaw digging into your chest,
So hard to retain your calm
When your fingernails are making serious alterations in
    your life line or love line or some other important
    line in your palm;
So hard to give your usual effect of cheery benignity
When you know your position is one of the two or
    three in life most lacking in dignity.
And your mouth is like a section of road that is being
    worked on,
And it is all cluttered up with stone crushers and con-
    crete mixers and drills and steam rollers and there
    isn't a nerve in your head that you aren't being
    irked on.
Oh, some people are unfortunate enough to be strung
    up by thumbs,
And others have things done to their gums,
And your teeth are supposed to be being polished,
But you have reason to believe they are being demol-
    ished,
And the circumstance that adds most to your terror
Is that it's all done with a mirror,

Because the dentist may be a bear, or as the Romans used to say, only they were referring to a feminine bear when they said it, an ursa,

But all the same how can you be sure when he takes his crowbar in one hand and mirror in the other he won't get mixed up, the way you do when you try to tie a bow tie with the aid of a mirror, and forget that left is right and vice versa?

And then at last he says That will be all; but it isn't because he then coats your mouth from cellar to roof

With something that I suspect is generally used to put a shine on a horse's hoof,

And you totter to your feet and think, Well it's all over now and after all it was only this once,

And he says come back in three monce.

And this, O Fate, is I think the most vicious circle that thou ever sentest,

That Man has to go continually to the dentist to keep his teeth in good condition when the chief reason he wants his teeth in good condition is so that he won't have to go to the dentist.

No, Mrs. Chutney, no, I am not going to Madison
    Square Garden,

I am not going to the dog show, and what do you think
    of that, and if you think what you probably think,
    I beg your pardon.

Some people like not listening to Bing Crosby and
    other people like not listening to Lawrence Tib-
    bett,

But I like not attending the annual canine exhibit.

The prizes are very nice, I am sure, and so are the
    donors,

And I guess the dogs are all right, but I'm afraid I can't
    stand the owners,

Because some of them breed dogs for love and some
    for riches,

But my experience has been that most of them do it
    just so they can startle their friends at the dinner
    table and the drawing room by babbling with self-
    conscious and unconsciousness about bitches,

So back, Mrs. Chutney, back to your breeding and bea-
    gling,

I find you are very fatigueling;

You are one of the reasons why when somebody says
    dogs are people's best friends,

My esteem for them ends,

Because whenever I hear of somebody whose best friend
    has four feet,

Well, that is the person that I would stay away from in
    droves rather than meet.

I think dogs are wonderful in their place,

But I refuse to admit that they are a superior or equal
race;

I will not attribute to every precocious poodle or spaniel

The wisdom of a Daniel.

I know that some of them can count up to ten and
carry the newspaper home in their mouth and
stand upon their hind legs and waltz,

But so could I if I wanted to, so I am not thereby
blinded to their faults.

When they are wet they do not smell like a rose,

And when they are dry they shed all over your furniture and clothes,

Another thing dogs do, and indeed have been doing
from the days of Ulysses,

Is to turn all the authors who write about them into
great big sissies.

Whoever you read, be it Homer or Albert Payson Ter-
hune or Browning,

Their dogs do nothing but go around and be faithful
to people and mourn on people's graves and rescue
them from fire and drowning,

And I admit that this gives their pages a lovely lovable
flavor,

And maybe that actually is how dogs spend their time,
but all I can say is no dog has yet ever done me a
favor.

To make a long story short, in the words of Omar Khay-
yam,

I don't mean that I don't like dogs, I just want to say
that I don't think they are any better than I am.

There was a poet who asked out loud,
"O why should the spirit of mortal be proud?"
The which is a typical poet's question
Born of temper or indigestion,
For poets, when their affairs go wrong,
Take it out in satiric song;
If all on their own they fall from grace,
They blast the whole of the human race;
They resent, when mocked by a passport photo,
Not their face, but mankind in toto.
Poets believe in pixies and elves
And blaming everyone but themselves.
Such was the poet who asked out loud
"O why should the spirit of mortal be proud?"
A notable piece of rhymed invective,
Which proves the poet had no perspective.
His argument wins for the other side;
For the spirit of mortal should swell with pride
At producing the poet who asked out loud
"O why should the spirit of mortal be proud?"
The more annoyed that a poet gets,
The deeper he's buried in duns and debts,
The more he's flouted and jeered and jilted,
The further his cup of woe is tilted,
The more his liver is misbehaving,
The more that he cuts himself while shaving,
The further his collar buttons roll,
The blacker the clouds that shadow his soul,
Why, the greater his scorn for his fellow man,

And a wasp is what he is busier than;
Apoplexy he's on the brink of,
He writes the nastiest he can think of.
Yet the more that the world by him is scorned,
The more is the world by him adorned,
And the more at mortals he bites his thumbs,
The more immortal he becomes,
For people share through all creation
One weakness of the American nation;
The books they prize upon their shelves
Say the horridest things about themselves.
Is this fact hidden from the poet,
Or does the unscrupulous scribbler know it?

There is one thing that ought to be taught in all the col-
leges,

Which is that people ought to be taught not to go
around always making apologies.

I don't mean the kind of apologies people make when
they run over ou or borrow five dollars or step on
your feet,

Because I think that kind is sort of sweet;

No, I object to one kind of apology alone,

Which is when people spend their time and yours apol-
ogizing for everything they own.

You go to their house for a meal,

And they apologize because the anchovies aren't caviar
or the partridge is veal;

They apologize privately for the crudeness of the other
guests,

And they apologize publicly for their wife's housekeep-
ing or their husband's jests;

If they give you a book by Dickens they apologize because it isn't by Scott,

And if they take you to the theater, they apologize for
the acting and the dialogue and the plot;

They contain more milk of human kindness than the
most capacious dairy can,

But if you are from out of town they apologize for
everything local and if you are a foreigner they
apologize for everything American.

I dread these apologizers even as I am depicting them,

I shudder as I think of the hours that must be spent in
    contradicting them,

Because you are very rude if you let them emerge from
    an argument victorious,

And when they say something of theirs is awful, it is
    your duty to convince them politely that it is mag,
    nificent and glorious,

And what particularly bores me with them,

Is that half the time you have to politely contradict
    them when you rudely agree with them,

So I think there is one rule every host and hostess ought
    to keep with the comb and nail file and bicarbonate
    and aromatic spirits on a handy shelf,

Which is don't spoil the denouement by telling the
    guests everything is terrible, but let them have the
    thrill of finding it out for themself.

I'd like to be able to say a good word for parsley, but
    I can't,

And after all what can you find to say for something
    that even the dictionary dismisses as a biennial
    umbelliferous plant?

Speaking of which, I don't know how the dictionary
    figures it as biennial, it is biennial my eye, it is like
    the poor and the iniquitous,

Because it is always with us, because it is permanent and
    ubiquitous.

I will not venture to deny that it is umbelliferous,

I will only add that it is of a nasty green color, and
    faintly odoriferous,

And I hold by my complaint, though every cook and
    hostess in the land indict me for treason for it,

That parsley is something that as a rhymer I can find
    no rhyme for it and as an eater I can find no reason
    for it.

Well, there is one sin for which a lot of cooks and
    hostesses are some day going to have to atone,

Which is that they can't bear to cook anything and
    leave it alone.

No, they see food as something to base a lot of beauti-
    ful dreams and romance on,

Which explains lamb chops with pink and blue pants on.

Everything has to be all decorated and garnished

So the guests will be amazed and astarnished,

And whatever you get to eat, it's sprinkled with a lot
    of good old umbelliferous parsley looking as limp
    and wistful as Lillian Gish,

And it is limpest, and wistfulest, and also thickest, on
    fish.
Indeed, I think maybe one reason for the disappearance
    of Enoch Arden
Was that his wife had an idea that mackerel tasted bet-
    ter if instead of looking like mackerel it looked like
    a garden.
Well, anyhow, there's the parsley cluttering up your
    food,
And the problem is to get it off without being rude,
And first of all you try to scrape it off with your fork,
And you might as well try to shave with a cork,
And then you surreptitiously try your fingers,
And you get covered with butter and gravy, but the
    parsley lingers,
And you turn red and smile at your hostess and com-
    pliment her on the recipe and ask her where she
    found it,
And then you return to the parsley and as a last resort
    you try to eat around it,
And the hostess says, Oh you are just picking at it, is
    there something wrong with it?
So all you can do is eat it all up, and the parsley along
    with it,
And now is the time for all good parsleyphobes to come
    to the aid of the menu and exhibit their gumption,
And proclaim that any dish that has either a taste or an
    appearance that can be improved by parsley is ipso
    facto a dish unfit for human consumption.

LINES TO BE SCRIBBLED ON SOMEBODY
ELSE'S THIRTIETH MILESTONE

Thirty today? Cheer up, my lad!
The good old thirties aren't so bad.
Life doesn't end at twenty-nine,
So come on in, the water's fine.
I, too, when thirty crossed my path,
Turned ugly colors with shame and wrath.
I kicked, I scratched, I bit my nails,
I indulged in tantrums the size of whales,
I found it hard to forgive my mater
For not having had me ten years later.
I struggled with reluctant feet
Where dotage and abdomens meet.
Like the tongue that seeks the missing tooth
I yearned for my extracted youth.
Since then some years have ambled by
And who so satisfied as I.
The thirties are things I wallow among,
With naught but pity for the young.
The less long ago that people were born
The more I gaze on them with scorn,
And each Thanksgiving I Thanksgive
That I'm slowly learning how to live.
So conquer, boy, your grief and rage,
And welcome to the perfect age!
I hope good fairies your footsteps haunt,
And bring you everything you want,
From cowboy suits and Boy Scout knives,
To beautiful, generous, wealthy wives.

If you play the horses, may you play good horses,
If you want divorces, may you get divorces,
Be it plenty of sleep, or fortune, or fame,
Or to carry the ball for Notre Dame,
Whatever it is you desire or covet,
My boy, I hope you get it and love it.
And you'll use it a great deal better, I know,
Than the child that you were a day ago.

LITTLE MISS MUFFET SAT ON A PROPHET —
AND QUITE RIGHT, TOO!

I am sure that if anybody into the condition of hu-
    manity cares to probe,
Why they will agree with the prophet Job,
Because the prophet Job said that man that is born of
    woman is of few days and full of trouble, that's
    what was said by the prophet Job,
And the truth of that statement can be confirmed by
    anybody who cares to probe.
So you would think that being born to trouble and woe,
    man would be satisfied,
And indeed that just by being born at all his passion
    for trouble would be gratisfied.
But is man content to leave bad enough alone?
Not so, he has to go out and create a lot more trouble
    and woe of his own.
Man knows very well that rheumatism and measles and
    ice and fog and pain and senility and sudden death
    are his for the asking, and, indeed, his whether he
    asks for them or not,
But when it comes to agony, man is a glutton and a
    sot,
His appetite for punishment is immense,
And any torture that Nature overlooked, he invents.
There is no law of Nature that compels a man to drink
    too much,
Or even to think too much,
And when Nature looked at her handiwork, for pur-
    poses of her own she certainly added gender to it,

But she didn't order everybody to dive overboard and
surrender to it,
Yes, it may have been Nature who induced two people
to love each other and end up by marrying each
other,
But it is their own idea when they begin to lovingly tor-
ment and harry each other.
And it may have been Nature who developed the
mosquito and the gnat and the midge,
But man developed golf and bridge,
And Nature may have thought up centipedes and ants,
But man all by himself thought up finance,
So this prophet will utter just one utterance instead of
uttering them like the prophet Job in baker's
twelves,
Which utterance is that people could survive their natural trouble all right if it weren't for the trouble
they make for themselves.

I trust I am not a spoil sport, but there is one thing I
    deplore,
And that is a party next door,
If there is anything that gives me tantrums galore
It is a party next door.
I do not know how we came into this world, or what
    for,
But it was not, I am sure, to listen to a party next door.
I am by nature very fond of everybody, even my neigh-
    bors,
And I think it only right that they should enjoy some
    kind of diversion after their labors,
But why don't they get their diversion by going to the
    movies or the Little Theater or the Comédie
    Française or the Commedia dell'arte?
Why do they always have to be giving a party?
You may think you have heard a noise because you have
    heard an artillery barrage or an avalanche or the
    subway's horrendous roar,
But you have never really heard anything until you
    have heard a party next door.
You may have survived the impact of a gangster's bullet
    or a hit-and-run driver or a bolt of lightning or the
    hammer of Thor,
But you really don't know what an impact is until you
    have felt the impact of a party next door.
A party next door never really gets going until you are
    trying for some much-needed sleep,

And when it does get going, why awake is much easier
   than your temper to keep.
At a party next door the guests stampede like elephants
   in wooden shoes and gallop like desperate polo
   players,
And all the women are coloratura sopranos and all the
   men are train announcers and hogcallers and saxo-
   phone solo players.
They all have screamingly funny stories to tell to each
   other,
And half of them get at one end of the house and half
   of them get at the other end of the yard and then
   they yell to each other.
The spirit is one of lawlessness and mockery,
And its audible symbols are giggles and squeals and guf-
   faws and splintering furniture and crashing crock-
   ery.
And even if the patrolman looks in from his beat they
   do not moderate or stop,
No, they just seduce the cop.
And at last you manage to doze off by the dawn's early
   light,
And they wake you up all over again shouting good
   night,
And the host roars out to people to come back in for
   a final cup,
And the windows rattle with horns blowing for wives
   who can't find their bags, and engines being warmed
   up,

And whether it consists of two quiet old ladies drop-
    ping in for a game of bridge or a lot of revelers get-
    ting really sort of out-of-bounds-like,
That's what a party next door always sounds like,
So when you see somebody with a hoarse voice and a
    pallid face and eyes bleary and red-rimmed and
    sore,
It doesn't mean they've been on a party themselves, no,
    it probably means that they have experienced a
    party next door.

HARK! HARK! THE PARI-MUTUELS BARK!

I

Willow waley and woe and sorrow,
The horses are coming to town tomorrow.
Chestnut and bay and black and gray
Sport and cavort and snort and neigh.
The horses, the horses are on the way!
The horses are coming to town tomorrow,
And some must beg and others borrow.
The horses are coming, enter the horses,
Exit the remnant of my resources,
Here goes me, and never a doubt of it,
And the horses don't even get anything out of it.
They don't get money or love or fun,
Why in the world must the horses run?
Or if they must, through a fate unholy,
Why must some of them run so slowly?
Brothers, the country's crying need
Is horses that run at an equal speed
And a stone-dead heat on every track
And every one getting their money back.
Willow waley and woe and sorrow,
The horses are coming to town tomorrow.
Every horse with a personal grudge
Against this modestly hopeful judge,
Holding its life as cheap as a song
If its death in the stretch should prove me wrong.
Well listen horses, I know you hate me,
But do not think to intimidate me,

Or drive from the track, by deed or threat,
The man who has never cashed a bet.
One day I shall hold a winning ticket,
And swagger up to the teller's wicket,
And take my money and catch a boat
To the land of the horsemeat table d'hôte.
Oh, I'll sit in Paris till Doomsday breaks
Chewing over my old mistakes.

II

O, racing is a ruinous sport,
The race track is an ill resort,
My waxing poverty I owe to it,
I often wonder why I go to it;
I hate the horses I have bet on,
I hate the horses my heart is set on;
Some are outsiders, some are sure things,
But if mine own, are ever poor things.
I hate the hunches, I hate the dope,
I hate the fear, I hate the hope,
I hate the blinkers, I hate the wrappers,
I hate the trainers and handicappers,
I hate the dust, I hate the mud,
I hate the pulsation of sporting blood,
I hate the jumps, I hate the flat,
And the red-hot tips from the stable cat,
The silly saddles, the foolish stirrups,
And the hang-arounders' cheerful chirrups,
The inhuman machines and human bookies,
And the plungers with faces like man-eating cookies,

The rattle and drum of the pounding hoof,
The triumphant shout that rocks the roof.
I hate my horse to be out in front
Lest he should wilt beneath the brunt;
I hate to see my horse behind,
Lest he be trapped in a pocket blind,
And when my horse is in the center,
The hooks I hang upon are tenter,
And oh, the microphones that retch
And tell you who's leading in the stretch!
Into your helpless ear they quack
Who's moving up, who's falling back,
Your fingers would find their gullets, if
From tearing up tickets they weren't so stiff
I mean it when I feelingly state
That racing is my bitterest hate.
But of all emotions within the breast,
Hate is by far the ugli-est.
To ugly hate I will not yield,
But bet five dollars on the field.

My attention has been recently focussed
Upon the seventeen year locust.
This is the year
When the seventeen-year locusts are here,
Which is the chief reason my attention has been
    focussed
Upon the seventeen-year locust.
Overhead, underfoot, they abound,
And they have been seventeen years in the ground,
For seventeen years they were immune to politics and
    class war and capital taunts and labor taunts,
And now they have come out like billions of insect
    debutantes,
Because they think that after such a long wait,
Why they are entitled to a rich and handsome mate,
But like many another hopeful debutante they have
    been hoaxed and hocus-pocussed,
Because all they get is another seventeen-year locust.
Girl locusts don't make any noise,
But you ought to hear the boys.
Boy locusts don't eat, but it is very probable that they
    take a drink now and again, and not out of a
    spring or fountain,
Because they certainly do put their heads together in
    the treetops and render Sweet Adeline and She'll
    Be Comin' Round the Mountain.
I for one get bewildered and go all hot and cold
Everytime I look at a locust and realize that it is seven-
    teen years old;

It is as fantastic as something out of H. G. Wells or
     Jules Verne or G. A. Henty
To watch a creature that has been underground ever
     since it hatched shortly previous to 1920,
Because locusts also get bewildered and go hot and cold
     because they naturally expected to find Jess Wil-
     lard still the champion,
And Nita Naldi the vampion,
And Woodrow Wilson on his way to Paris to promote
     the perpetually not-yet-but-soon League,
And Washington under the thumb of Wayne B.
     Wheeler and the Anti-Saloon League.
Indeed I saw one locust which reminded me of a god-
     motherless Cinderella,
Because when it emerged from the ground it was whis-
     tling Dardanella.
Dear locusts, my sympathy for you is intense,
Because by the time you get adjusted you will be de-
     funct, leaving nothing behind you but a lot of
     descendants who in turn will be defunct just as
     they get adjusted seventeen years hence.

There are some people who if you say something nice
    to them,
They certainly don't encourage you to do it twice to
    them,
Because you pay them a compliment and they are not
    receptive and gracious,
No, they snub you as if you had said something in-
    sulting and outracious.
You say Isn't that a becoming dress!
And they say What, this mess?
And you say something like This evening your eyes
    are very beautiful, and the only reason you say it
    is that you think this evening their eyes are very
    beautiful,
And they promptly inform you that they know that
    you really think their eyes look like two incom-
    patible poached eggs, and are just saying the other
    to be dutiful.
Or maybe you tell your favorite author that their last
    book seems to you one of the best things since
    Pickwick or the Koran,
And their answer implies that either you are a liar, or,
    if you really liked it, you would probably have to
    study night and day for years even to get to be a
    moron.
Come on Modesty, step up and take the blame;
Thou art responsible, Modesty, for all the innocent
    little compliments strangled in thy name.

And there is one thing of which it might be well to remind the gruff rebuffer,

Which is that beauty is in the eye of the beholder, and the complimenter may indeed have been mistaken, because to somebody else maybe the dress *was* a mess, and the eyes *were* like two incompatible poached eggs, and the book *was* spiritless trash composed by an octogenarian duffer;

Because everybody who has somebody who thinks they are wonderful also has somebody who thinks they are terrible,

And all I wish the rebuffers is that they may overhear the conversation of their enemies if they find the conversation of their friends so unbearable.

I know a renegade hotel.
I also know I hate it well.
An inn so vile, an inn so shameless,
For very disgust I leave it nameless,
Loathing the name I will not utter,
Whose flavor reeks of rancid butter.
Five stories tall this mantrap stands,
With steps outstretched like welcoming hands,
And travelers, weary of their mileage,
Respond to its bright electric smileage.
They park their cars, and praise the Lord
For downy bed and toothsome board.
They pass unwary through its portals,
And every imp in Hades chortles.
Behold the regulars in the lobby;
Expectoration is their hobby.
Behold the loftiest of clerks:
He's manicuring as he works,
And bridles into dapper wrath
At a mild request for a room and bath.
Behold the niftiest of collars
Which murmurs, "That will be six dollars,"
The leer with innuendo rife,
Which says your wife is not your wife.
The doddering, halting elevator,
A contemporary of Poe or Pater.
The impudent boy with step that lags
Who snatches your coins and hides your bags;

The ill-fitting door to the musty room
That smells like a fairly empty tomb;
The bath you crave, being cramped and dusty
And the hot that turns out to be cold and rusty,
The towels clammy, the basin black,
And the bed that sags like a postman's back.
The dinner (two dollars and a quarter)
For the porterhouse that tastes like the porter.
The sleepy ascent to the room once more,
And the drunken Lothario next door,
Alone, and not wishing to be alone
Who roars his loves to the telephone.
You see that the beds are not turned down,
And you know the bedclothes are dank and brown,
And there isn't a thing to hang your clothes on,
And the sheet you shudder to place your toes on.
You search in vain for a bedside lamp,
You lose your slippers, the rug is damp,
The bulb in the ceiling is all in all,
And the switch is set in the furtherest wall.
A century later the night is past,
And you stagger down to break your fast.
Octoroon coffee, and shiny eggs
Semi-equipped with beaks and legs.
And you reach the desk and surrender your keys,
And the clerk sneers "Thirteen dollars, please,
Seven for meals and six for the room,
Do you know to who you are speaking to whom?
You can fry in Hell so long as you pay;

Stop in again when you pass our way!"
I know a renegade hotel.
I also know I hate it well.
I'd name its name with my hand on the Bible,
But for disgust. And the laws of libel.

THE NAME IS TOO FAMILIAR

You go away for a trip, either business or pleasure,

And you think to settle down to a little anonymous
leisure,

And the first thing you see on the train is a sign bearing
the name of the porter,

And his name is Lafcadio Pauncefoote so you can't
call him Boy or George, which eventually worries
you into giving him an extra quarter,

And you go into the dining car a little later,

And there you are confronted with signs confiding to
you the names of the steward and the waiter,

And the steward hovers over you like a hospitable owl,

And you can't call him Steward because now you think
of him as Mr. Feeney your host, so when he asks
you how your steak is you say Splendid instead of
Foul,

And you get off the train and into a taxi,

And there's a picture to tell you that the driver's name
is Maxie,

And you don't want to be hemmed in by names, you
want to be alone,

But you think, At least it's other people's names that
are hounding me and not my own,

And you go and register at a hotel and up comes the
third assistant manager with a third assistant man-
agerial gurgle,

And he looks at the register and then shakes hands and
says We're mighty glad to have you with us, Mr.
Alf B. Murgle,

We certainly hope you enjoy your stay, Mr. Murgle,

And the bellboy gets the idea and says Right this way, Mr. Murgle,

And the elevator boy gets the idea and says This is your floor, Mr. Murgle,

And the floor clerk gets the idea and says Good morning Mr. Murgle, there's your door, Mr. Murgle,

And the telephone girl gets the idea and says, Good morning Mr. Murgle, okay Plaza 3–8362, Mr. Murgle,

And the waiter gets the idea and says Will that be all, Mr. Murgle? Thank you, Mr. Murgle,

So your private life in the hotel is about as private as the private life of the Dionnes, but at first you are slightly flattered because you think Somebody important must have sent them word of you,

And after they have Mr. Murgled you for the thousandth time you try to cash a two-dollar check and you discover they have never heard of you,

Yes, it's all a figure of speech,

Because they not only know you, but also don't know you, and combine the worst features of each.

That's the beauty about a name, whenever we want to anonymously relax it pops up and prevents us,

And it is certainly nice to get home again and settle down as an obscure statistic in the census.

On the fair face of life there obtrudes one major excrescence.

Oh! you say, I know, it is sickness. Well that's just what you know wrong, it isn't sickness at all, it's convalescence.

Not that sickness is eighteen-karat tutti frutti,

But at least it legalizes various lapses from dutti,

And it makes you feel temporarily important,

Which is well worth the fear that by it your life may be shortent,

Because you feel heroic like a hero out of Alger or Henty,

And a couple of degrees of fever are as stimulating as two drinks and as soporific as twenty,

With the result that there is something definitely pleasing

About a little mild diseasing,

But that only strengthens my conviction that there is something definitely distressing

About convalescing.

Convalescence is the period

When compensations are lacking but irritations are myriad;

It is the time when you are reduced to reading your wife's fashion magazines because you have finished every book on every shelf;

It is the time when everybody is tired of you, but that is nothing compared to how tired you are of yourself;

It is the time when of lassitude you have a surplus;

The time when you are convinced you will never be
well again, but all your friends and relatives are
convinced either that you never were sick at all, or
if you were you got sick deliberately, or on pur-
plose;

When you have to prop your eyes open during the
afternoon,

And you sink gratefully on your bed at night and then
lie tossing until finally the sun comes up and you
sink into an uncomfortable swoon;

It is the time when your complexion is yellow with just
perhaps a soupçon of green,

And whatever room you wander into you seem to put
your foot in some part of the household routine,

And then the doctor comes for a final inspection and
what does he say?

Well he passes you as fit for starting work again but
warns you against frolic and play;

Yes, he says you are in fine fettle for things like writing letters and paying bills,

But anything in the nature of frivolity will only bring
a return of your various ills;

So at last your patience reaches the breaking point,

And your rebelliousness reaches the waking point,

And you leap from your wheel chair or sun bath or
whatever it is with a cry of Boo!

And you rush into the great world and whatever is on
your mind, you do.

And there may have been times when you felt burlier,

But your only regret is that you didn't break jail a week
    earlier,
Because whatever happens is a blessing,
Because whether it kills you or cures you, at least you
    are through with convalescing.

There is one phase of life that I have never heard dis
    cussed in any seminar,
And that is that all women think men are funny and
    all men think that weminar.
Be the air the air of America or England or Japan,
It is full of husbands up in it saying, Isn't that just like
    a woman? And wives saying, Isn't that just like a
    man?
Well, it so happens that this is a unique fight,
Because both sides are right.
Although I must say, while the opportunity is season-
    able,
That I do think that women would rather be right than
    be reasonable.
But anyhow each sex keeps on laughing at the other
    sex for not thinking the way they do,
Which is the cause of most domestic to-do and a-do,
Because breakfast is punctuated with spousely snorts,
Because husbands are jeering at their wives because
    they ignore the front page and read society and
    fashions, and wives are jeering at their husbands
    because they ignore the front page and read finance
    and sports,
And women think it is ridiculous of men to spend their
    spare time reading a book or catching a fish or
    wielding a racquet or a putter, or getting tattooed,
And men think it is ridiculous of women to spend
    their spare time talking about other women who
    aren't there, or going from shop to shop trying

everything on and not intending to buy anything,
    or getting manicured or shampooed.
And men also think that women have an easy time be-
    cause all they have to do is look after the house-
    hold,
And what does that amount to but keeping an eye on
    the children and seeing that three meals a day
    are served and not allowing any litter to collect
    that would furnish a foothold for a mousehold?
And women also think that men have an easy time be-
    cause all they have to do is sit in an office all day
    long swapping stories and scratching up desks with
    their heels,
And going out to restaurants and ordering everything
    they like for their midday meals.
And there is one special point on which couples can
    never agree when they think,
And that is, how much is enough to drink.
And oh yes, women like to resent the thought that they
    think men think they are toys,
And men like to bask in the thought that they think
    women think they are just big overgrown boys.
Well all these conflicting thoughts make for trouble
    at times but on the whole it is a sound idea for
    men and women to think different,
It is a topic upon which I am verbose and vociferant,
Because who was it who wrote of the miserable town
    where the girls were too boisterous and the boys
    were too girlsterous, was it Damon Runyon,
Or could it have been John Bunyan?

Well anyhow, that author had a gifted pen;
Because who would want to live in a world where the
     men all thought like women and the women all
     thought like men?
No, no, kind sirs, I will take all my hard-earned money,
And I will bet it on the nose of the tribe whose men
     and women continue to think each other are funny.

THE BANQUET

Oh, here we are at the mammoth banquet
To honor the birth of the great Bosanquet!
Oh give a look at the snowy napery,
The costly flowers, the sumptuous drapery,
Row on row of silver utensils
Poised for action like salesmen's pencils,
Waiters gaudy as sugar plums,
Every waiter with seven thumbs,
Stream upon stream of gaudy bunting,
And lady commuters lion hunting,
The gleaming teeth at the speaker's table,
The clattering, chattering, battering babel.
Sit we here in the great unquiet
And brood a while on the evening's diet.
As soggy and dull as good advice,
The butter floats in the melting ice.
In a neighboring morgue, beyond salvation,
The celery waits identification.
Huddled thick in an open vault,
Mummified peanuts moult their salt.
Out of the napkin peers a roll,
With the look of a lost and hardened soul.
The cocktail sauce, too weak to roister,
Fails to enliven the tepid oyster.
The consommé, wan as Elizabeth Barrett,
Washes over a drowning carrot.
Next, with its sauce of Mdvi-Tarter,
The sole, or flounder, or is it a garter?
Ho! fresh from the ranchos of Avignon,

O'Sullivan's Rubber filet mignon;
Parsley potatoes, as tempting as soap,
String beans, hemp beans, and beans of rope.
And the waiter would sooner serve you his daughter
Than give you another glass of water.
Pineapple salad next, by George!
That ought to raise your sunken gorge!
And green ice cream, sweet frozen suet,
With nuts and raisins sprinkled through it.
At sight of vari-colored gâteaux
The innards reel, as on a bateau.
At last the little cups belated
Of coffee dated, or inundated.
Chairs creak as half a thousand rumps
Twist them around with backward bumps.
A thousand eyes seek out, as one,
The beaming chairman on his throne.
He rises luminous through the smoke
Of banquet tobacco, or poison oak.
He bows, he coughs, he smiles a bit,
He sparkles with imitable wit —
Rabbi Ben Ezra, fly with me;
The almost worse is yet to be.
Let us arise and leave this banquet —
And by the way, Rabbi, who was Bosanquet?

DO SPHINXES THINK?

There is one thing I do not understand,
Which is how anybody successfully cuts the fingernails
    on their right hand,
Because it is easy to cut your left-hand fingernails, but
    with your right-hand fingernails, why you either
    have to let them grow ad infinitum,
Or else bitum.
Then there is another problem that keeps my brain
    working in two twelve-hour shifts,
Which is Why doesn't the fact that everything that
    goes up must come down, apply to elevators, or
    as the Americans say, lifts?
You have been standing on the tenth floor waiting to
    descend to the ground floor since Bob Son of
    Battle was a pup,
And all you see is elevators going up, up, up,
And first your impatience, and eventually your curiosity,
    grows keen,
When you see the same elevator going up a dozen
    times without having been down in between.
Is there a fourth dimension known only to elevator
    attendants,
Or do they, when they get to the top, glide across the
    roof to the next building and there make their
    descendance?
Whatever the secret is, to know it I should adore,
For I am tired of being marooned without my ten
    favorite movie actresses on the tenth floor.

An answer to the third baffler, however, would make
    the greatest difference in this dear old life o' mine,
Which is, ought I to hope to feel terrible, or to feel
    fine?
Because how can I tell which hope to nurse,
Because when I feel terrible I know that after a while
    I'll feel better, and when I feel fine I know that after
    a while I'll feel worse.
Is it better to feel terrible and know that pretty soon
    you'll feel fine or to feel fine and know that
    pretty soon you'll feel terrible, that is the ques-
    tion,
And I am open to suggestion,
And when you consider further that probably nobody
    can ever feel either fine or terrible anyhow, because
    how can you feel fine when you know that you're
    going to feel terrible or how can you feel terrible
    et cetera it all grows very confusing,
So let's leave everything in the hands of Dorothy Dix
    and Ted Husing.

WEDNESDAY MATINEE

Oh, yes, I'd love to go to the play,
But not the Wednesday matinee.
I'd rather stay home with Lorna Doone
Than go of a Wednesday afternoon,
I'd rather work on a crumbling levee
Than cope with a Wednesday theater bevy.
Women, women, and still more women;
A sea of drugstore perfume to swim in;
Tongues like sirens, and tongues like clappers,
And the ripping crackle of candy wrappers:
(A fudge-nut sundae was all their lunch,
They are dying for something sweet to munch;)
And foreheads grow moist and noses glisten,
It's everyone talk, and nobody listen;
Voice beats on voice, and higher and higher
Screams and steams the anarchic choir.
The early-comers sit on the aisle
With their laps in a Himalayan pile,
Every corpulent knee a sentry
Denying to all the right of entry.
The usher glances at laps and knees,
And murmurs, Show me your tickets, please.
The aborigines clatter and clack,
But they're next aisle over and eight rows back.
Thither they march, with candy and wraps,
To be balked by other knees and laps.
The house lights fade, the footlights glow,
The curtain rises. This is the show;

This is the charm, the enchanted flame,
That drew them here from wherever they came.
Over the house no silence falls,
But shopper to shopper desperate calls;
Suburban ladies their tonsils gird,
Determined to have one final word,
Interrupting their own ripe rush
To squelch their neighbors with cries of Hush!
The dialogue dies upon the stage
At the rustle and swish of the program page.
With a wave of applause, terrific, tidal,
They recognize the star, their idol,
Undeterred by the sober fact
That she doesn't appear till the second act.
Now the whisper runs from row to row,
Doesn't the butler look like Joe?
And the mother's the image of Emily, kind of,
And who does the lover put you in mind of?
Now, like the drunkard scenting liquor,
The ladies sniff for dirt, and snicker;
Forgetting now their gum and fudge,
The ladies cackle and leer and nudge,
Rooting in every harmless line
For double-entendre and obscene design;
Yet prompt with handkerchief and tears
The moment a child or a dog appears.
The curtain falls; the play is ended.
Adorable! Dreadful! Stupid! Splendid!
They cry of the play that was unattended,
Unheard, unseen, and uncomprehended.

O matinee mænads, O bulging bacchantes,
I would my pen were as sharp as Dante's,
But as it isn't I simply say
You may keep your Wednesday matinee.

Fish are very good at swimming,
And the ocean with them is brimming.
They stay under water all year round,
And they never get drowned,
And they have a gift more precious than gold,
Which is that they never get cold.
No, they may not be as tasty as venison or mooseflesh,
But they never get gooseflesh.
They have been in the ocean since they were roe,
So they don't have to creep into it toe by toe,
And also they stay in it permanently, which must be
    a source of great satisfaction,
Because they don't have to run dripping and shivering
    up and down the beach waiting vainly for a
    healthy reaction.
Indeed when I think how uncomplicated the ocean is
    for fish my thoughts grow jealous and scathing,
Because when fish bump into another fish it doesn't
    wring from them a cry of Faugh! and ruin their
    day's bathing.
No, if it's a bigger fish than they are, they turn around
    and beat it,
And if it's littler, they eat it.
Some fish are striped and some are speckled,
But none of them ever heard of ultra-violet rays and
    felt it necessary to lie around getting sand in their
    eyes and freckled.

Oh, would it not be wondrous to be a fish? No, it
would not be wondrous,
Because we unmarine humans are at the top of the
animal kingdom and it would be very undignified
to change places with anything under us.

Come, megrims, mollygrubs and collywobbles!
Come, gloom that limps, and misery that hobbles!
Come also, most exquisite melancholiage,
As dark and decadent as November foliage!
I crave to shudder in your moist embrace,
To feel your oystery fingers on my face.
This is my hour of sadness and of soulfulness,
And cursed be he who dissipates my dolefulness.
The world is wide, isn't it?
The world is roomy.
Isn't there room, isn't it,
For a man to be gloomy?
Bring me a bathysphere, kindly,
Maybe like Beebe's,
Leave me alone in it, kindly,
With my old heebie-jeebies.
I do not desire to be cheered,
I desire to retire, I am thinking of growing a beard,
A sorrowful beard, with a mournful, a dolorous hue
    in it,
With ashes and glue in it.
I want to be drunk with despair,
I want to caress my care,
I do not wish to be blithe,
I wish to recoil and writhe,
I will revel in cosmic woe,
And I want my woe to show.
This is the morbid moment,
This is the ebony hour.

Aroint thee, sweetness and light!
I want to be dark and sour!
Away with the bird that twitters!
All that glitters is jitters!
Roses, roses are gray,
Violets cry Boo! and frighten me.
Sugar is diabetic,
And people conspire to brighten me.
Go hence, people, go hence!
Go sit on a picket fence!
Go gargle with mineral oil,
Go out and develop a boil!
Melancholy is what I brag and boast of,
Melancholy I mean to make the most of,
You beaming optimists shall not destroy it.
But while I am it, I intend to enjoy it.
Go, people, feed on kewpies and soap,
And remember, please, that when I mope, I mope!

COMPLAINT TO FOUR ANGELS

Every night at sleepy-time
Into bed I gladly climb.
Every night anew I hope
That with the covers I can cope.

Adjust the blanket fore and aft,
Swallow next a soothing draught;
Then a page of Scott or Cooper
May induce a healthful stupor.

O the soft luxurious darkness,
Fit for Morgan, or for Harkness!
Traffic dies along the street.
The light is out. So are your feet.

Adjust the blanket aft and fore,
Sigh, and settle down once more.
Behold, a breeze! The curtains puff.
One blanket isn't quite enough.

Yawn and rise and seek your slippers,
Which, by now, are cold as kippers.
Yawn, and stretch, and prod yourself,
And fetch a blanket from the shelf.

And so to bed again, again,
Cozy under blankets twain.
Welcome warmth and sweet nirvana
Till eight o'clock or so mañana.

You sleep as deep as Keats or Bacon;
Then you dream and toss and waken.
Where is the breeze? There isn't any.
Two blankets, boy, are one too many.

O stilly night, why are you not
Consistent in your cold and hot?
O slumber's chains, unlocked so oft
With blankets being donned or doffed!

The angels who should guard my bed
I fear are slumbering instead.
O angels, please resume your hovering;
I'll sleep, and you adjust the covering.

Solomon said, Stay me with apples for I am sick with
 l'amour,
But I say, Comfort me with flagons, for I am sick with
 rich people talking and acting poor.
I have never yet met even a minor Crœsus
Whose pocketbook didn't have paresis;
I have never yet been out with a tycoon for an evening
 in Manhattan's glamorous canyons
When the evening's bills weren't paid by the tycoon's
 impoverished but proud companions.
There is one fact of life that no unwealthy child can
 learn too soon,
Which is that no tycoon ever spends money except on
 another tycoon.
Rich people are people that you owe something to and
 take out to dinner and the theater and dancing
 and all the other expensive things there are because you know they are accustomed to the best
 and as a result you spend the following month on
 your uppers,
And it is a big evening to you but just another evening
 to them and they return the hospitality by saying
 that someday you must drop in to one of their cold
 Sunday suppers.
Rich people are also people who spend most of their
 time complaining about the income tax as one of
 life's greatest and most intolerable crosses,
And eventually you find that they haven't even paid

any income tax since 1929 because their income
has shrunk to fifty thousand dollars a year and
everything has been charged off to losses,
And your own income isn't income at all, it is salary,
and stops coming in as soon as you stop laboring
mentally and manually,
But you have been writing out back-breaking checks
for the Government annually,
So the tax situation is just the same as the entertain-
ment situation because the poor take their little
pittance
And pay for the rich's admittance
Because it is a great truth that as soon as people have
enough coupons in the safe-deposit vault or in
the cookie-jar on the shelf,
Why they don't have to pay anything themself,
No, they can and do just take all their coins and store
them,
And other people beg to pay for everything for them
And they certainly are allowed to,
Because to accept favors is the main thing that the
poor are and the rich aren't too proud to,
And I think this is wrong and I say Heave-ho my
hearties,
Let's make everybody we know who is richer than we
are give a lot of parties
Let us make it a Federal offense
For rich people not to be as spendthrift as a Federal
agency and give everybody a big time and hang
the expense.

The only danger of this plan is that if it went through
    the rich people wouldn't be rich any more,
Because the reason they get rich and stay rich is be-
    cause not to spend money is the chief thing they
    adore,
But nevertheless let us face this contingency with sang-
    froid and phlegm,
And I propose a Twenty-second Amendment to the
    Constitution providing that the rich must spend as
    much money on us poor as we do on them.

They are constantly getting themselves bedizened,
And they say it is you they are doing it for, but it isn't.
Oh no, dear fellow male, it has nothing whatsoever
    to do
With either me or you,
Because if it was only a question of doing it for us,
The bedizening would require fewer feathers and much
    less fuss.
Oh yes, they say they bedeck themselves to make them-
    selves attractive to their mate, potential or actual,
But I am afraid that that statement of theirs is not
    factual,
Because if there is one thing about which they are not
    reverential,
It is any opinion of their clothes expressed by their
    mate, actual or potential,
And any mate venturing to express any such opinion
Soon finds himself less than a minion,
And this is a statement which can really be put to the
    touch,
Because just remember the last time that yours wore
    something that you admired specially much,
And you had a lot of enthusiastic praise and were not
    sparing of it,
And said Oh what a lovely dress, and hoped there would
    be frequent wearing of it,
Because it was a dress of which you were very fond,
And you thought it the most becoming she had ever
    donned.

Yes, and what was the result?

The dress was never again seen because some other
kind of dress was immediately decreed by the
couturier's cult.

And that's what happens to the clothes that she would
still be looking marvelous in if her claim that she
dresses just to please you had any validity,

But any male who comments on the fact becomes about
as popular around the house as asafœtidity,

So then she goes out and buys a garment with the lines
of a birthday cake or a hat worn by a royalty of
Britain,

And the only way you can explain anybody's buying it
is that when they boughten it they were litten,

And you are asked how you like it, and you either say or
don't say, depending on your daring,

But whatever you say it doesn't make any difference because it's going to be worn because it's what all
the other women are wearing,

Because a woman's mental processes are harder to understand than those of a cannibal or an angel or an
elf,

And they would rather dress like every other woman
and look terrible than dress differently and look
beautiful as their own beautiful self.

A PLEA FOR A LEAGUE OF SLEEP

Some people lead a feverish life,
For they with restlessness are rife.
They revel in labors energetic,
Their fare is healthful and ascetic,
Their minds are keen, their hands are earthy,
Each day they work on something worthy.
Something accomplished, something done,
Comprises their idea of fun.

My life with joy is sometimes fraught,
But mostly when I'm doing naught.
Yea, I could spend my whole career
A pillow underneath my ear.
How wise was he who wittily said
That there is nothing like a bed.
A mattress is what I like to creep on;
The left side is the one I sleep on.

Heroes who moil and toil and fight
Exist on eight hours' sleep a night.
I call this but a miserly budget,
Yet I assure you that they grudge it.
I've heard them groan, times without number,
At wasting a third of their lives in slumber.
All right, you Spartans who build and delve,
You waste eight hours, and I'll waste twelve.

No honester man is to be found
Than he who sleeps the clock around.

Of malice and ambition free,
The more he sleeps, the sleepier he.
No plots and schemes infest his head,
But dreams of getting back to bed.
His spirit bears no worldly taint;
Scratch a sluggard, and find a saint.

Stalin and Hitler while they sleep
Are harmless as a baby sheep;
Tyrants who cause the earth to quake
Are only dangerous when awake.
This world would be a happier place,
And happier the human race,
And all our pilots be less Pontius,
If people spent more time unconscious.

CAPTAIN JOHN SMITH

Captain John Smith
Didn't belong to the B'nai B'rith,
He was a full-blooded Briton,
The same as Boadicea and Bulwer-Lytton,
But his problem and theirs were not quite the same,
Because they didn't have to go around assuring every-
   body that that was their real name,
And finally he said, This business of everybody raising
   their eyebrows when I register at an inn is getting
   very boring,
So I guess I'll go exploring,
So he went and explored the River James,
Where they weren't as particular then as they are now
   about names,
And he went for a walk in the forest,
And the Indians caught him and my goodness wasn't
   he emborrassed!
Yes, his heart turned to plasticene
Because he certainly was the center of a nasty scene,
And he was too Early-American to write for advice from
   Emily Post,
So he prepared to give up the ghost,
And he prayed a prayer but I don't know whether it
   was a silent one or a vocal one,
Because the Indians were going to dash his brains out
   and they weren't going to give him an anaesthetic,
   not even a local one,
But along came Pocahontas and she called off her
   father's savage minions,

Because she was one of the most prominent Virginians,
And her eyes went flash flash,
And she said, Scat, you po' red trash,
And she begged Captain John Smith's pardon,
And she took him for a walk in the gyarden,
And she said, Ah reckon ah sho' would have felt bad
    if anything had happened to you-all,
And she told him about her great-uncle Hiawatha and
    her cousin Sittin' Bull and her kissin' cousin King
    Philip, and I don't know who-all,
And he said you'd better not marry me, you'd better
    marry John Rolfe,
So he bade her farewell and went back to England,
    which adjoins Scotland, where they invented golf

REQUIEM

There was a young belle of old Natchez
Whose garments were always in patchez.
When comment arose
On the state of her clothes,
She drawled, When Ah itchez, Ah scratchez!

The only people who should really sin
Are the people who can sin with a grin,
Because if sinning upsets you,
Why, nothing at all is what it gets you.
Everybody certainly ought to eschew all offences however venial
As long as they are conscience's menial.
Some people suffer weeks of remorse after having committed the slightest peccadillo,
And other people feel perfectly all right after feeding their husbands arsenic or smothering their grandmother with a pillow.
Some people are perfectly self-possessed about spending their lives on the verge of delirium tremens,
And other people feel like hanging themselves on a coathook just because they took that extra cocktail and amused their fellow guests with recitations from the poems of Mrs. Hemans.
Some people calmly live a barnyard life because they find monogamy dull and arid,
And other people have sinking spells if they dance twice in an evening with a lady to whom they aren't married.
Some people feel forever lost if they are riding on a bus and the conductor doesn't collect their fare,
And other people ruin a lot of widows and orphans and all they think is, Why there's something in this business of ruining widows and orphans, and

they go out and ruin some more and get to be
    a millionaire.

Now it is not the purpose of this memorandum, or
    song,

To attempt to define the difference between right and
    wrong;

All I am trying to say is that if you are one of the un-
    fortunates who recognize that such a difference
    exists,

Well, you had better oppose even the teensiest temp-
    tation with clenched fists,

Because if you desire peace of mind it is all right to do
    wrong if it never occurs to you that it is wrong
    to do it,

Because you can sleep perfectly well and look the world
    in the eye after doing anything at all so long as you
    don't rue it,

While on the other hand nothing at all is any fun

So long as you yourself know it is something you
    shouldn't have done.

There is only one way to achieve happiness on this
    terrestrial ball,

And that is to have either a clear conscience, or none
    at all.

You ask me, brothers, why I flinch.
Well, I will tell you, inch by inch.
Is it not proper cause for fright
That what is day will soon be night?
Evenings I flinch the selfsame way,
For what is night will soon be day.
At five o'clock it chills my gore
Simply to know it isn't four.
How Sunday into Monday melts!
And every month is something else.
If Summer on the ladder lingers,
Autumn tramples upon her fingers,
Fleeing before the jostling train
Of Winter, and Spring, and Summer again.
Year swallows year and licks its lips,
Then down the gullet of next year slips.
We chip at Time with clocks and watches;
We flee him in love and double scotches;
Even as we scatter in alarm
He marches with us, arm in arm;
Though while we sleep, he forward rides,
Yet when we wake, he's at our sides.
While grandly paying no attention to us
He's doing things I hate to mention to us.
His the chain letter never broken;
For each, each day he leaves some token;
Let men walk straight or let them err,
He never leaves them as they were.
While ladies draw their stockings on

The ladies they were are up and gone.
I pen my lines, I finish, I scan them,
I'm not the poet who began them.
Each moment Time, the lord of changers,
Stuffs our skins with ephemeral strangers.
Good heavens, how remote from me
The billion people I used to be!
Flinch with me, brothers, why not flinch,
Shirts caught in the eternal winch?
Come, let us flinch till Time stands still;
Although I do not think he will.
Hark brothers, to the dismal proof:
The seconds spattering on the roof!